Feast of Italy

Feast of Italy

300 Illustrations in Color

Translated from the Italian edition published by
Arnoldo Mondadori Editore

Thomas Y. Crowell Company
New York   Established 1834

Copyright © 1973 by ARNOLDO MONDADORI EDITORE

Originally published in Italy under the title *Cucina all'Italiana,*
© 1972 by ARNOLDO MONDADORI EDITORE.

Consulting Chef: GIORGIO GIOCO
Photographs by PINO DAL GAL

Printed in Italy

ISBN 0-690-00059-6

Library of Congress Cataloging in Publication Data
Main entry under title:

Feast of Italy.

    Translation of Cucina all'Italiana.
     1. Cookery, Italian. I. Mondadori (Arnoldo)
editore.
TX723.F413   641.5′945   73-3118
ISBN 0-690-00059-6

Contents

Antipasti

Antipasti have never played a very important part in Italian cookery, unlike cooking in other European countries. Nevertheless, as a result of cooking having become more international, antipasti are enjoying a revival in Italy. Because a pasta dish or a risotto limit the choice of an antipasto, it tends to become an alternative choice.

To the ancient Romans antipasti consisted basically of eggs, olives, spiced sausages, lettuce, seafood and fine shellfish sauces. With a few exceptions Italian antipasti have remained the same as those of ancient Roman cookery, but the choice of vegetables and fish has widened and today we have a wide range from sliced ham to soft salamis or the matured salamis which are typical of this sphere of cookery. A basic characteristic of the antipasto should be the lightness of the food, and this rule is especially observed when the prince of Italian antipasti is served: two thin slices of raw lean ham.

Some of the ingredients used in this section are not always to be found in the United States. Where possible suitable alternatives have been suggested. Squid, for example, can be used instead of cuttlefish.

SARDINE RELISH

GOURMET'S SQUID

(Sardine in Saor)   **Serves 6**

2¼ pounds fresh sardines	2 carrots, cut in julienne
6 tablespoons flour	1 clove garlic, crushed
sunflower seed oil for frying	2 bay leaves
salt	pepper
1 onion, thinly sliced	6 tablespoons olive oil
1 celeriac, cut in julienne	½ cup vinegar (heated)

(Calamari Ghiottone)   **Serves 6**

6 medium squid	1 tomato, finely chopped
chopped basil	6 tablespoons olive oil
chopped parsley	salt and pepper
¼ onion, chopped	½ cup dry white wine
1 clove garlic, chopped	

(This is a Venetian dish. The highly flavored marinade enables one to keep large quantities of fish for several days.)

Scale, gut and wash the sardines and dry them carefully on a napkin. Dip them in flour and fry in the sunflower seed oil in a skillet. Drain them on absorbent paper and, while still hot, sprinkle them with salt. Dip the vegetables in flour and fry them in the oil used for the sardines. Place the fried fish and vegetables in alternate layers in a deep oven-proof dish. Add the garlic, bay leaves and pepper; sprinkle with olive oil and the heated vinegar. Cover the dish and keep it in a cool, but not cold, place.

Cut out the eyes and mouth of the squid. Remove the ink sac and internal bone. Cut off the tough points on the tentacles. Rub off the skin and wash under running water until white. Cut the tentacles from the sac and mince these finely with the basil, parsley, onion, garlic and tomato. Mix and season with oil, salt and pepper; stuff the sacs of the squid wtih this mixture. Close the opening of the sacs to retain the stuffing by sewing or skewering with a toothpick which can be removed later. Place the stuffed sacs in an oven-proof dish, sprinkle with additional oil and bake in a preheated 450°F. oven for 30 minutes. While the squid are cooking, sprinkle them with white wine and season again with a little salt and pepper. Serve them cold with antipasto, garnishing the fish with chopped parsley.

| **SQUID SALAD** | **MUSSELS WITH BASIL** |

(Insalata di Seppie)   Serves 6

¾ pound white squid
1 teaspoon **salt**
¼ cup vinegar
6 tablespoons olive oil
   juice of 1 lemon
   salt and pepper

1 clove garlic (inner bud removed)
   chopped parsley
   black olives
   red peppers
   lemon quarters

(Cozze al Basilico)   Serves 6

1 pound mussels
   basil leaves
1 clove garlic

6 tablespoons olive oil
   pepper

Cut out the eyes and mouth of the squid. Remove the ink sac and internal bone. Cut off the tough points on the tentacles. Rub off the skin and wash under running water until white. Pound the meat to tenderize it. Submerge the prepared squid in a saucepan of boiling water, to which 1 teaspoon salt and ¼ cup vinegar have been added. Cover with a lid and simmer for about 1 hour. Before removing from the heat, prick the meat with a fork to ensure that it is properly cooked. Drain, cool and cut into strips. Sprinkle with the oil, lemon juice, salt and pepper, garlic and the chopped parsley. Serve in shells garnished with black olives, slices of red peppers and quartered lemons.

Wash, scrub and "beard" the mussels. Spread them out in a large skillet lightly greased with oil, together with 3 to 4 of the basil leaves and the garlic. Place the pan over high heat to allow the shells to open. Remove the mussel meat and serve it on the half shell on a shell-shaped dish. Sprinkle with oil, pepper and a few spoonfuls of the strained mussel stock left in the skillet. Garnish with a sprinkling of freshly chopped basil.

OCTOPUS WITH GARLIC

TUNA FISH, CUBAN STYLE

(Polipi Veraci all'Aglio)   **Serves 6**

2 octopus (about 1½ pounds each)
¼ cup olive oil
5 cloves garlic, crushed
1 bay leaf

½ teaspoon cumin seeds
  salt
1 small green pepper, chopped
  rosemary leaves and parsley

(Tonno alla Cubana)   **Serves 6**

6 tuna steaks, ½ pound each
6 tablespoons flour
6 tablespoons olive oil
1 onion, thinly sliced
1 bunch celery, cut in julienne
1 carrot, cut in julienne

2 tablespoons pickled pearl onions
1 tablespoon capers
¼ cup white raisins
1 cup pine nuts
1 red pepper, cut in strips
  salt

Cut out the eyes and mouth of the octopus. Remove the ink sac and internal bone. Cut off the tough points on the tentacles. Put each octopus on a board and beat them well to break the fibers and make the meat more tender. Wash them in running water until they are very white; do not dry, but put them in an earthenware dish and season with oil, flavored with garlic, bay leaf and cumin seeds. Cover the dish tightly with a sheet of waxed paper or foil tied around the top with string. Put the dish over very low heat between 1 and 2 hours, according to the size of the octopus. When they are tender, drain them, season with additional oil, salt, green pepper, rosemary leaves and parsley. Serve in a tureen.

Wash and clean the tuna steaks and dredge them in flour. Place them in the oil in a large skillet over low heat, turning carefully to brown on both sides. Then add the onion, celery, carrot, pickled onions, capers, white raisins, pine nuts and red pepper. Season with salt, add ½ cup hot water and put in a preheated 350° F. oven for about 10 minutes or until the flesh flakes with a fork. Put the hot tuna and the sauce from the pan in an oven-proof dish and serve with a salad.

BLACK OLIVES WITH ANCHOVIES

A SALAD APPETIZER

(Olive Nere all'Acciuga)   Serves 6

1¼ pounds black olives	4 anchovy fillets
½ onion, chopped	oregano
1 clove garlic, chopped	¾ cup olive oil

(Insalata Appetitosa)   Serves 6

5 tomatoes	1 can (1 pound) tuna fish in oil
4 hard cooked eggs	10 anchovy fillets
1 can (7 ounces) green Spanish olives	black Gaeta olives
	salt and pepper
1 yellow or red pepper	½ cup olive oil
1 green pepper	

If possible use an olive pitter to remove the pits from the olives carefully and cleanly. Prepare the sauce by gently simmering the onion, garlic, anchovy fillets and the oregano in oil in a saucepan. Cook for about 5 minutes, then strain the sauce through a sieve over the olives. Decorate the dish according to taste and offer as a predinner appetizer.

Wash the tomatoes and then cut almost in half. Cut the eggs into wedges. Pit the olives, trying to keep the flesh as whole as possible. Clean the peppers, singe over the burner to loosen the skins and peel them. Remove the seeds and cut peppers into strips. Turn the tuna fish out onto a crystal plate and decorate the top of it with some of the anchovy fillets and egg wedges. Arrange the Spanish olives, green peppers, tomatoes and the remaining anchovy fillets around it. Surround with more egg wedges and black Gaeta olives and garnish with the yellow or red pepper. Add salt and pepper to the olive oil and spoon over the salad.

STUFFED TOMATOES

ONION OMELETTE

(Pomodori Farciti)   Serves 6

6 ripe tomatoes	6 tablespoons olive oil
salt	pepper
chopped parsley	6 slices Fontina cheese
chopped basil	
1 clove garlic (inner bud removed), chopped	

(Frittata con Cipollotti)   Serves 6

3 large onions, sliced	salt and pepper
4 tablespoons butter	¼ cup vinegar
8 eggs	

Choose tomatoes of the same size. Wash them well, cut off the tops and, using a teaspoon, remove the seeds, pulp and juice. Lightly salt the insides and leave them standing upside down on a rack to drain the insides completely. Prepare a stuffing of parsley, basil and garlic and season with oil and pepper. (Do not use salt, as the tomatoes have already been salted.) Fill the tomatoes with this mixture. Place them closely together, but not touching, in a greased oven-proof dish in a preheated 450° F. oven for about 5 minutes. At the end of this time put a slice of Fontina cheese on each tomato; leave them in the oven for another 10 minutes. Serve hot, garnished with basil leaves and parsley sprigs.

Parboil the sliced onions in boiling salted water for a few minutes. Drain well and simmer in a saucepan with butter. Beat the eggs in a bowl, adding salt and pepper; pour them over the onions which have been well spread out over the bottom of the saucepan. When the eggs have become firm turn the omelette out on a hot round metal plate and sprinkle with vinegar.

TASTY POLENTA

MOZZARELLA WITH OREGANO

(Polenta Condita)   **Serves 6**

5 cups water
1 tablespoon salt
3 cups cornmeal

12 slices Gorgonzola cheese
12 slices Fontina cheese
½ cup white wine
7 tablespoons melted butter

(Mozzarella all'Origano)   **Serves 6**

3 ripe tomatoes
3 pounds mozzarella cheese
6 tablespoons olive oil

salt and pepper
oregano
basil leaves

Bring the salted water to a boil. When it is boiling rapidly, slowly add the cornmeal, mixing constantly with a whisk to avoid lumping. When the meal is well mixed in, cook it over high heat for 1 hour, stirring with a wooden spoon constantly. Turn it out onto a wide board and let it stand for 20 minutes. Cut the polenta into 12 even slices with a wire or sharp, thin knife. Place the slices in an earthenware baking dish greased with butter. On each piece of polenta place a slice of Gorgonzola and a slice of Fontina. Sprinkle with wine and melted butter and put in a preheated 450° F. oven until the wine has evaporated and the cheese has melted. Serve straight from the cooking dish as shown above.

If you can obtain fresh, white firm mozzarella and sun-ripened tomatoes, you can prepare a delicious summer antipasto. Choose tomatoes of the same size, wash well, dry and polish; cut into slices lengthwise, leaving the slices joined at the base. Open them in a fan shape, widening each section with a knife blade, and insert a slice of the delicate milky cheese between each of the sections; or slice the mozzarella and the tomatoes and put alternate layers of each on a floral serving dish. In either case, season with oil, salt, pepper and oregano and decorate with basil leaves.

TUSCAN TOAST

BREAD SOUP

(Crostini alla Toscana)   Serves 6

1 clove garlic (inner bud removed)	salt and pepper
½ onion, chopped	sage to taste
4 tablespoons butter	1 bottle (2½ ounces) capers,
8 chicken livers, finely chopped	drained and finely chopped
	12 slices bread, toasted

(Pan Bagnato)   Serves 6

3 gherkins, finely sliced	1 onion, sliced
8 slices stale homemade style	few leaves basil, chopped
bread	½ cup olive oil
¼ cup vinegar	salt and pepper
4 ripe tomatoes, cut in wedges	5 hard cooked eggs, cut in wedges

Sauté garlic and chopped onion lightly in the butter in a small saucepan. Sauté the livers for a few minutes, only until they lose their pinkness. Add the salt, pepper and sage, and the chopped capers; mix well. Spread this pâté over the slices of toasted bread or squares of bread browned in the oven. Serve warm either as an appetizer or as a garnish for roast chicken.

Place the sliced gherkins in a small bowl and cover them with a weighted plate for 10 minutes. Drain off the excess water and wash. Place the slices of stale bread in the bottom of a soup tureen and sprinkle them with vinegar. Season the tomatoes, onion and basil with oil, salt and pepper. Spread them over the bread with the wedges of egg and gherkin slices. Put in the refrigerator and serve ice cold.

HEARTS OF PALM SALAD

ANTIPASTO ITALIAN STYLE

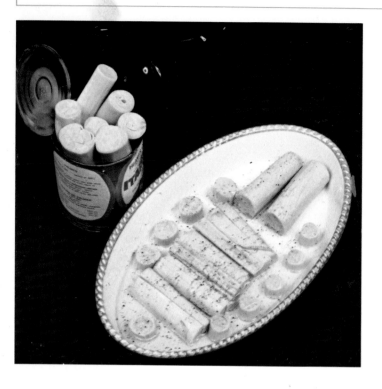

(Cuori di Palma)   **Serves 6**

1 can (1 pound) hearts of palm	pepper
¼ cup olive oil	4 anchovy fillets, chopped
juice of ½ lemon	chopped parsley

(Antipasto all'Italiana)   **Serves 6**

6 slices San Daniele ham	6 slices Lombardy salami
6 slices coppa	18 curls butter
6 slices raw Parma ham	12 baby artichokes in oil
6 slices cooked Valtellina ham	black Gaeta olives
6 slices Bologna mortadella	green Spanish olives

Remove the hearts of palm from the can and drain them. Cut some lengthwise and some into rings. Arrange these on an earthenware dish. To make the sauce, add the oil, lemon juice and pepper to the chopped anchovies. Pour the sauce over the hearts of palm, sprinkle with chopped parsley and serve.

(These are the traditional ingredients; not all are available in the United States. Some that are—prosciutto, coppa, boiled ham, Italian salami, black olives and ripe green olives.)

Arrange the meat slices attractively on a round white earthenware serving dish. Prepare curls of butter with a butter curler and place them over the meat as a decoration; or cream some butter until fluffy and pipe a design over the meat. Open each artichoke to a flower shape and place them around the plate, together with black and green olives.

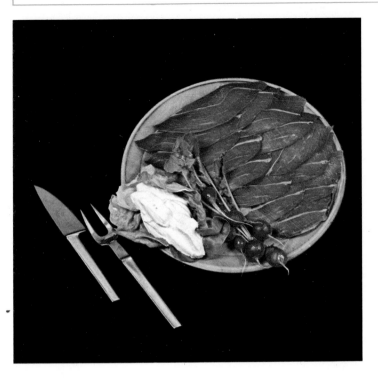

(Speck al Cren)   Serves 6

18 slices speck   pinch salt
3 small bunches radishes   1 teaspoon sugar
1 horseradish   ½ cup heavy cream

(Prosciutto e Melone)   Serves 6

2 melons   12 slices prosciutto ham

(Speck is not available in the United States, but we have substituted prosciutto.)

Slice the speck thinly and place on a brightly colored serving dish. Decorate with a cluster of red radishes and serve with a horseradish sauce prepared as follows: Scrape the skin from the horseradish and then grate the juicy pulp into a bowl. Add the salt and sugar and mix. In another bowl lightly whip the cream until it is thick but still does not peak. Gently fold the cream into the horseradish with a spoon.

Choose medium-sized ripe melons. Cut the melon in slices and remove the seeds. Cut between the rind and flesh on each slice but leave them attached at one end. Reserve a few slices of the prosciutto and spread the remainder on a plate. Wrap the reserved slices of prosciutto around some of the melon slices and arrange the melon around the ham. This dish looks very attractive served on a yellow plate with a touch of green added.

SALAMI AND FIGS

MELON WITH WHITE WINE

(Sopressa e Fichi)   Serves 6

18 slices salami   lettuce leaves
12 figs

(Melone al Vino Bianco)   Serves 6

3 melons   ¼ cup dry sherry
3 cups dry white wine

An antipasto of salami and figs is always very attractive and tempting. This tasty sausage and sweet summer figs make a good combination. Put the slices of salami in the center of a brightly colored serving dish and arrange broad lettuce leaves alongside. Score the fig skins lengthwise in four or five places. Starting from the top of the fig and following the cut, detach the skin in sections from the flesh but leave attached at the base. Arrange the skin like the petals of a flower with the fruit in the center. The flavor of the figs is best if served very cold straight from the refrigerator.

Choose medium-sized ripe melons. Cut a small piece off each end so the melon halves will stand evenly. Cut the melons in half. Using a small spoon, remove the seeds from each half melon, and cut out little melon balls with a melon scoop. Put these balls in a bowl, cover with the wine and sherry and put into refrigerator to marinate. Lightly sugar the insides of the melon halves and put them into the refrigerator for 2 hours to chill. Shortly before serving, fill the empty melon halves with the melon balls and sprinkle them with the liquid left in the bowl in which they have been standing. Serve the half melons on lettuce leaves or on leaf-shaped green-glazed plates.

In spite of the restrictions required by modern diets, pasta dishes still play an important part in Italian cookery. There are two stages in the preparation of pasta dishes—the cooking and the seasoning. The rules for cooking pasta are firmly defined and are handed down by tradition and experience. The seasoning, on the other hand, is often a matter of personal inspiration; the flavors and seasonings are mingled with the distinctive quality of an impromptu creation. Spaghetti, the most important of all the numerous types of pasta, combined with tomato sauces gives an immediate pleasure and satisfaction for its mouth-watering visual appeal.

SPAGHETTI WITH GARLIC AND OIL   SPAGHETTI, AMERICAN STYLE

Photo Barilla

Photo Barilla

(Spaghettini Aglio e Olio)   **Serves 4 to 6**

1 pound thin spaghetti	freshly ground pepper
¼ cup olive oil	chopped parsley
3 cloves garlic (inner buds removed), crushed	

(Spaghetti all'Amatriciana)   **Serves 4 to 6**

8 slices bacon, diced	3 or 4 medium tomatoes, peeled, seeded and drained
3 tablespoons cooking oil	salt
small green chili pepper, chopped	1 pound spaghetti
½ onion, chopped	grated Romano cheese

Cook the spaghetti in plenty of boiling salted water. Drain it when it is *al dente* (firm to the bite); place on a heated serving dish. Meanwhile put the oil and crushed garlic into a small saucepan to heat. Sauté the garlic over high heat, removing it as soon as it becomes golden brown. Pour the hot, seasoned oil over the pasta and sprinkle with freshly ground pepper and chopped parsley.

Sauté the diced bacon in oil over high heat. When the bacon is golden brown, remove it from the oil with a slotted spoon and keep it hot. Sauté the green pepper and chopped onion in the same oil until lightly browned. Add the drained tomatoes to the sauce. (The quantity of tomatoes may be adjusted according to how much juice they contain.) Season with a little salt and cook the sauce for 10 minutes (it should not be red, but light pink in color). Add the reserved bacon to the sauce. At the same time cook the spaghetti in plenty of boiling salted water. Drain it when it is *al dente* (firm to the bite). Put the spaghetti into a deep warm serving dish and pour the hot sauce over it. Mix in the 6 tablespoons of grated Romano cheese. Serve immediately accompanied with additional grated Romano cheese.

SPAGHETTI WITH VEGETABLES

(Spaghetti alla Giardiniera)   **Serves 4 to 6**

2 green peppers	⅓ pound button mushrooms, sliced
1 onion, chopped	½ pound lima beans, shelled
1 clove garlic (inner bud removed), crushed	1 pound green peas, shelled
	salt and pepper
7 tablespoons butter	½ cup dry red wine
½ cup olive oil	1 pound tomatoes, peeled
1 package (10 ounces) frozen artichoke hearts, defrosted	1 pound spaghetti
	¾ cup grated Parmesan cheese

Turn the peppers on a fork over a medium flame until charred. Peel or rub off the skin, halve and remove the seeds. Wash and cut the peppers into strips. Sauté the chopped onion and crushed garlic in the saucepan with the butter and oil. When the onion and garlic are golden brown, add the green peppers, artichoke hearts, mushrooms, beans and peas. Season with salt and pepper and add the red wine. When the wine has partially evaporated, add the tomatoes. Cover the saucepan and let the sauce simmer. Cook the spaghetti in plenty of boiling salted water. Drain when the spaghetti is *al dente* (firm to the bite) and turn out into a hot serving dish. Cover with the vegetable sauce. Serve accompanied with grated Parmesan cheese.

SPAGHETTI WITH CLAM SAUCE

Photo Barilla

(Spaghetti alle Vongole)   **Serves 4 to 6**

1 pound clams, scrubbed	salt and pepper
¾ cup olive oil	chopped parsley
2 cloves garlic (inner buds removed), crushed	freshly ground pepper
	1 pound spaghetti
1¼ pounds tomatoes, peeled	

Put the clams in a saucepan with ¼ cup oil and heat. When the clams open, remove them from the heat and quickly detach the meat from the shells. Reserve the meat. Strain the stock in the saucepan through a fine sieve and set it aside. Sauté the garlic in a pan with the remaining oil. Remove the garlic when it has become golden brown and discard it. Add the tomatoes to the oil, season with salt and pepper and simmer until the juice of the tomatoes has evaporated. When the sauce has thickened, add the clams and the strained stock. Simmer briefly to warm through, then add the chopped parsley, an extra dash of olive oil and some freshly ground pepper. Meanwhile cook the spaghetti in plenty of boiling salted water until it is *al dente* (firm to the bite). Drain and turn into a warm bowl. Serve the clam sauce over the spaghetti.

SAVORY SPAGHETTI

ADRIATIC SPAGHETTI

Photo Barilla

(Spaghetti Saporiti) **Serves 4 to 6**

1 onion, chopped	2 tablespoons tomato purée
1 stalk celery	¼ cup dry white wine
parsley	salt and pepper
rosemary	1 pound spaghetti
5 sage leaves	6 tablespoons Parmesan cheese
12 anchovy fillets	6 tablespoons grated Romano
½ cup olive oil	cheese

Mince the onion, celery, parsley, rosemary, sage and anchovies together. Heat the oil in a saucepan; brown, stirring with a wooden spoon. Dilute the tomato purée with the wine and add to the mixture. Add salt and pepper, but be careful, as the anchovies are salty. Reduce the heat to moderate and let the sauce simmer. Meanwhile, cook the spaghetti in plenty of boiling salted water until it is *al dente* (firm to the bite). Drain and turn onto a warm serving dish. Mix in the sauce and grated Parmesan and Romano cheeses.

(Spaghetti dell'Adriatico) **Serves 4 to 6**

1 small octopus (about 3¼ pounds)	1 green chili pepper, chopped
½ cup olive oil	½ pound tomatoes, peeled and cut
pinch rosemary	in strips
1 bay leaf	3 cloves garlic (inner buds removed), chopped
pinch oregano	
1 teaspoon cumin seeds	salt and pepper
chopped parsley	1 pound spaghetti

The octopus must be very carefully washed and dried, and the mouth removed. Cover the bottom of a saucepan with oil; add the rosemary, bay leaf, oregano, cumin seeds, parsley, chili pepper, tomatoes and chopped garlic. Place the octopus on top of this mixture and season with salt and pepper. Cover the pot very tightly and simmer for about 45 minutes. Cook the spaghetti in plenty of boiling salted water until it is *al dente* (firm to the bite). Drain and turn onto a warm serving dish. Mix the octopus sauce into the spaghetti. Serve piping hot.

SAN GIOVANIELLO VERMICELLI

SPAGHETTI WITH MUSSEL SAUCE

Photo Barilla

(Vermicelli alla San Giovaniello)　　　　**Serves 4 to 6**

1 pound vermicelli	4 basil leaves
3¼ pounds tomatoes, peeled, seeded, sliced and drained	20 pitted black olives, quartered
	12 anchovy fillets, chopped
½ cup olive oil	2 teaspoons capers, washed and drained
salt and pepper	

(Spaghetti al Sugo di Mare)　　　　**Serves 4 to 6**

4½ pounds mussels	½ teaspoon rosemary
¾ cup olive oil	½ bay leaf
2 cloves garlic (inner buds removed), chopped	1 pound tomatoes, peeled
	½ green chili pepper, chopped
⅛ teaspoon oregano	salt
2 tablespoons chopped parsley	1 pound spaghetti

Break the strands of vermicelli into thirds. In a saucepan alternate layers of tomatoes with layers of vermicelli and season with oil, salt, pepper, basil, quartered black olives and chopped anchovies until all the ingredients are used up, finishing with a layer of tomatoes. The vermicelli should cook in the sauce. If there is insufficient sauce to cover the vermicelli, add a little stock. Cover the saucepan and cook over high heat for at least 15 minutes. When ready, the vermicelli should be firm and just covered with the sauce. Serve the vermicelli and sauce in a heated oven-proof dish, topped with capers.

Wash, scrub and "beard" the mussels. Put them in a large saucepan with ¼ cup oil. Heat them over high heat to open, but do not cook. Take from the heat and remove the flesh; reserve. Strain the mussel stock from the saucepan through a sieve and reserve. Brown the garlic in the remaining oil with the oregano, parsley, rosemary and bay leaf. Let these cook for a minute to bring out the flavor, then add the tomatoes, chopped chili pepper and salt. Simmer the sauce slowly; when it has reduced a little, add the mussels, leaving the pan over the heat for a few minutes. Cook the spaghetti in plenty of boiling salted water until it is half cooked. Drain and turn into an earthenware bowl. Add the sauce and the reserved mussel stock. Place the dish in a preheated 375° F. oven for about 20 minutes or until the spaghetti is fully cooked and the mussel stock absorbed. Serve straight from the oven.

Photo Barilla

(Spaghettini del Fattore)   Serves 4 to 6

¼ cup olive oil
1 clove garlic
1 cup (1 ounce) Italian dried
   mushrooms, soaked in warm water
   30 minutes, squeezed dry

5 tablespoons tomato purée
1 can (6 ounces) tuna fish in oil,
   flaked with a fork
   salt and pepper
1 pound thin spaghetti

(Vermicelli con Cipolline e Piselli)   Serves 4 to 6

10 small onions
 6 tablespoons butter
 2 slices bacon, diced
 1 cup shelled peas
 ½ teaspoon sugar
   pepper

2 tablespoons tomato purée
½ cup hot stock
  salt
1 pound vermicelli
⅔ cup grated Parmesan cheese
  chopped parsley

Heat oil in saucepan and sauté garlic lightly; discard garlic. Reserve the water from the mushrooms; then chop and sauté in the garlic-flavored oil. Add the reserved mushroom water, cover and simmer until the mushrooms are tender. Add the tomato purée and tuna fish. Grind a little pepper into the sauce and add a little salt (if needed—the tuna is inclined to be salty). Cook the spaghetti in plenty of boiling salted water until it is *al dente* (firm to the bite). Drain and turn into a hot serving dish. Cover with the tuna sauce.

Peel the onions and soak them in fresh water. Chop them and cook lightly in a saucepan with 3 tablespoons of the butter and the diced bacon. Cover and cook slowly, adding a little water if necessary. Add the peas, sugar, pepper and the tomato purée diluted with the hot stock. Increase the heat and cook quickly for about 20 minutes. Add the salt when the peas are cooked, in order to make them more tender and preserve their green color. Cook the vermicelli in plenty of boiling salted water until it is *al dente* (firm to the bite). Drain and mix with the remaining butter, which has been melted, together with a few tablespoons Parmesan cheese and a little of the sauce. Arrange attractively on a warm serving dish and pour on the remaining sauce. Garnish with chopped parsley and serve accompanied with the remaining grated Parmesan cheese.

VERMICELLI WITH HAM AND PEAS

Photo Barilla

(Vermicelli con Prosciutto e Piselli)   **Serves 4 to 6**

4 tablespoons butter	½ cup stock
⅛ pound boiled ham, diced	salt
¼ onion, chopped	1 cup dry white wine
1 pound peas, shelled	1 pound vermicelli
pinch sugar	1 cup grated Parmesan cheese
pepper	

Put the butter, the fattest part of the ham and the chopped onion in a saucepan. Cook over low heat so that the onion does not brown. Add the peas, sugar, a little pepper and the stock. Raise the heat to high and boil the mixture, stirring constantly, to cook the peas quickly. When the peas are almost tender, add the salt, wine and the remaining lean ham. Reduce the wine over high heat, then remove the pan and keep the contents warm. Cook the vermicelli in plenty of boiling salted water. Cook until *al dente* (firm to the bite). Drain and turn out onto bright plates. Toss with the ham and peas mixture. Serve accompanied with grated Parmesan cheese.

BAVETTINE WITH TOMATO SAUCE

Photo Barilla

(Bavettine al Pomodoro)   **Serves 4 to 6**

1¼ pounds ripe tomatoes, peeled, seeded and cut in strips	½ cup olive oil
salt and pepper	1 clove garlic
1 bunch parsley, chopped	1 pound narrow linguine
5 basil leaves	¾ cup grated Parmesan cheese

Drain the liquid from the tomatoes in a colander, adding the salt, pepper, chopped parsley and the basil leaves. Heat the oil in a saucepan and add the garlic. Discard the garlic when it is golden brown; add the tomatoes and herbs. Sauté for a short time only, keeping the shape of the tomatoes and not allowing them to become mushy. Cook the linguine in plenty of boiling salted water until it is *al dente* (firm to the bite). Drain and toss with the sauce and grated Parmesan cheese. Serve on warm plates.

Photo Barilla

Photo Barilla

(Fettuccine al Pesto)   **Serves 4 to 6**

1 clove garlic
1 tablespoon pine nuts
2 cups basil leaves
   salt
1 cup grated Romano cheese
   pinch of cayenne pepper

1 cup olive oil
¼ cup boiling stock
1 pound medium egg noodles
   pinch of bicarbonate of soda
½ cup cold water

(Tagliatelle in Salsa di Fegatini)   **Serves 4 to 6**

¾ pound chicken livers
3 tablespoons olive oil
2 tablespoons butter
½ onion
¾ pound tomatoes, peeled, seeded,
      chopped and drained
   salt and pepper

1 pound broad egg noodles
      (tagliatelle)
   pinch of bicarbonate of soda
½ cup cold water
4 tablespoons butter, cut in pieces
¾ cup grated Parmesan cheese

This recipe features a celebrated Genoese sauce which is tra-
ditionally ground in a mortar with a pestle.* Chop the garlic
and pine nuts together finely. Add the basil leaves and a little
salt (to retain the color of the basil) and continue chopping. Put
the chopped ingredients into a mortar; add the Romano
cheese, mix in a pinch of cayenne pepper and grind the mixture with the pestle. When it is reduced into a paste, turn it
into a larger bowl and slowly beat in the oil. Add the boiling
stock just before pouring the sauce over the noodles. Cook
the noodles in plenty of boiling salted water. Before removing
the noodles from the stove, add the bicarbonate of soda and
the cold water to keep them firm and well separated. Drain
the noodles and serve very hot in a dish with the sauce.

* Good results can be obtained by making the sauce in an electric blender.
Combine half of the olive oil with the rest of the ingredients and blend on low
speed until they have been reduced to a paste. Continue blending on low
speed, adding the remainder of the oil gradually.

Remove any traces of gall from the livers, wash well and cut
into tiny pieces. Heat the oil and butter in a small pan; add the
livers and the onion; discard the onion as soon as it is lightly
browned. Sauté the livers quickly until browned, then reduce
the heat and simmer, covered, for a few minutes. Add the tomatoes to the chicken livers. Season with salt and pepper and
continue to simmer slowly. Cook the noodles in boiling salted
water. Add the bicarbonate of soda while they are cooking.
Before draining the noodles, add the cold water. (The soda
and the cold water will help to make the noodles light.) Turn the
drained noodles into a hot, deep serving dish and mix with the
sauce, pieces of butter and grated Parmesan cheese.

TAGLIATELLE WITH SAUSAGE

TAGLIATELLE WITH MUSHROOM SAUCE

(Tagliatelle con Funghi e Salsiccia)   **Serves 4 to 6**

½ to ¾ pound button mushrooms or
  ⅔ cup (⅔ ounce) Italian dried
  mushrooms, soaked in warm
  water 30 minutes, squeezed
  dry (reserve liquid)
⅓ pound Italian sausages
5 tablespoons olive oil
1 clove garlic
¼ onion

salt and pepper
1 pound broad egg noodles
  (tagliatelle)
  pinch bicarbonate of soda
⅓ cup melted butter
  chopped parsley
¾ cup grated Parmesan cheese

(Tagliatelle in Salsa di Funghi)   **Serves 4 to 6**

¾ pound button mushrooms or 1¼ cups
  (1¼ ounces) Italian dried mushrooms, soaked in warm water 30
  minutes, squeezed dry
¾ pound tomatoes, peeled and seeded
¼ cup olive oil
¼ onion
1 clove garlic

salt and pepper
1 pound broad egg noodles
  (tagliatelle)
  pinch bicarbonate of soda
½ cup cold water
2 tablespoons melted butter
¾ cup grated Parmesan cheese

If using button mushrooms, wipe with a clean towel and slice. Using a fork, dip the sausages briefly in boiling water; slice. Heat the oil in a saucepan and lightly brown the garlic and the onion. Discard the garlic and onion; add the sliced sausages and mushrooms and salt and pepper. Sauté quickly for a few minutes, reduce the heat and add the reserved liquid from the mushrooms. Simmer slowly until the mushrooms are tender. Cook the noodles in plenty of boiling salted water until they are al dente (firm to the bite). Add the bicarbonate of soda as they cook to make them light and keep them separated. Drain and turn into a hot serving bowl with the melted butter and a few tablespoons of the grated Parmesan cheese. Toss the noodles gently with two wooden forks to make them lighter. Cover with the mushroom sauce and garnish with a handful of chopped parsley. Serve accompanied with remainder of the grated Parmesan cheese.

Wipe the button mushrooms with a clean towel and slice. (If using dried mushrooms, soak in lukewarm water 30 minutes before slicing.) Drain the tomatoes. Heat the oil in a saucepan and sauté the tomatoes with the onion and garlic; add the sliced mushrooms. Season with salt and pepper and sauté briskly for 1 minute; then cover, reduce the heat and simmer until the mushrooms are tender. Cook the noodles in plenty of boiling salted water, adding the bicarbonate of soda. Before draining, add the cold water—this lightens the noodles. Put the noodles in a round hot serving bowl with the melted butter and a few tablespoons of the grated Parmesan cheese. Toss gently with two wooden forks to lighten. Cover with the tomato and mushroom sauce. Serve accompanied with remainder of the Parmesan cheese.

GREEN NOODLES WITH FOUR CHEESES | GREEN NOODLES MARINARA

Photo Barilla

Photo Barilla

(Tagliatelle Verdi ai Quattro Formaggi)   Serves 4 to 6

¼ pound Swiss cheese, cubed	pinch bicarbonate of soda
¼ pound Fontina cheese, cubed	½ cup cold water
¼ pound mozzarella cheese, cubed	⅓ cup melted butter
1 cup heated milk	1 cup grated Parmesan cheese
1 pound green noodles	

(Tagliatelle Verdi alla Marinara)   Serves 4 to 6

1¼ pounds mussels	salt and pepper
½ cup olive oil	chopped parsley
¼ onion	1 pound green noodles
1 clove garlic (inner bud removed), crushed	pinch bicarbonate of soda
5 ripe tomatoes, peeled, seeded and chopped	½ cup cold water

Soak the cubed Swiss, Fontina and mozzarella cheeses in the heated milk for about 1 hour. The cheeses should soften but not melt. Cook the green noodles in plenty of boiling salted water, adding the bicarbonate of soda. Before draining, add the cold water to keep the pasta light, firm in texture and separated. Turn the drained noodles into a hot, oval oven-proof dish; sprinkle with the melted butter and a few tablespoons of the grated Parmesan cheese. Pour half of the cheese sauce onto the noodles and toss gently with two wooden forks. Pour the remaining sauce over the top and garnish with a sprinkling of grated Parmesan cheese. Serve accompanied with the remainder of the grated Parmesan cheese.

Wash, scrub and "beard" the mussels. Heat 1 tablespoon olive oil in a saucepan; add the mussels and cook over high heat until they open. Remove the flesh, reserving a few of the shells with flesh still in them. Strain the stock left in the saucepan and reserve it. Sauté the onion and garlic in the remaining oil. Add the chopped tomatoes, salt, pepper and the chopped parsley. Cook over high heat. When the sauce is blended and thickened, add the mussels and a few tablespoons of the reserved strained stock. Cover, reduce the heat and simmer. Cook the green noodles in plenty of boiling salted water with the soda. Before draining, add the cold water to make the noodles firm, green and separated. Toss the drained noodles with the sauce. Place them in a warm serving dish and garnish with a few mussels on the half shell. Grind some black pepper over the top.

LINGUINE WITH TUNA FISH SAUCE

(Lingue di Passero al Tonno)   Serves 4 to 6

4 tablespoons butter
2 tablespoons flour
1 cup dry white wine
¾ cup grated Parmesan cheese
1 can (7 ounces) tuna fish in oil, flaked
   with a fork

freshly ground pepper
1 pound wide linguine
   olive oil

Melt the butter in a saucepan over low heat; stir in the flour and let it brown slightly. Add the white wine gradually, stirring constantly. Simmer the sauce for 5 minutes, remove from heat and add the Parmesan cheese, flaked tuna and the freshly ground pepper. Cook the noodles in plenty of boiling salted water until *al dente* (firm to the bite). Drain and turn into a heated dish. Toss with a little olive oil and the tuna sauce. Serve immediately.

MACARONI PIE

(Timballo alla Ferrarese)   Serves 4 to 6

For the filling
¼ pound chicken giblets
¼ pound veal sweetbreads
4 cups (¼ pound) Italian dried mushrooms, soaked in water 30 minutes,
   squeezed dry
5 tablespoons butter
   salt and pepper

¼ cup dry white wine
3 tomatoes, sliced
1 pound macaroni
1 cup grated Parmesan cheese
1 cup meat sauce (page 41)
1 cup Béchamel sauce (page 212)

For the crust
2 cups flour
7 tablespoons butter
¼ cup sugar

   pinch salt
2 egg yolks beaten with 3 tablespoons water

To prepare the crust: grease a round, deep oven-proof dish and sprinkle it with a little flour. Make the dough for the crust and let stand for 1 hour. Roll it out ¼ inch thick and line the dish; reserve the rest of the crust for the top. **To prepare the filling:** Wash the chicken giblets well. Blanch the sweetbreads in boiling water for 5 minutes; plunge into cold water and when cool, remove any skin and membranes. Cut the softened mushrooms and meat into small dice. Heat 1 tablespoon of the butter in a saucepan and brown the meats lightly. Season and add the white wine; reduce, then add the tomatoes and the mushrooms. Cover and simmer slowly. Cook the macaroni in plenty of boiling salted water until *al dente* (firm to the bite). Drain and turn into a tureen. Toss well with the remaining butter (cut in small pieces), Parmesan cheese, meat sauce and Béchamel sauce. Put the mixture into the pastry-lined dish. Cover with a circle of pastry, flute and prick with a fork. Put the dish in a preheated 450° F. oven for 20 minutes or until the pastry is browned and leaves the sides of the dish.

GREEN LASAGNE WITH RICOTTA CHEESE   FETTUCCINE MOLD

Photo Barilla

Photo Barilla

(Lasagne Verdi alla Ricotta)   **Serves 6**

For the meat sauce
⅛ pound lean beef	1 tablespoon oil
⅛ pound pork	1 tablespoon butter
1 slice mortadella	salt and pepper
1 slice ham	¼ cup red wine
½ stalk celery	1½ cups canned tomatoes or 2
½ carrot	large ripe tomatoes
½ onion	

For the filling
1¼ cups ricotta or cottage cheese	1 pound green lasagne
salt and pepper	3 tablespoons melted butter
pinch nutmeg	¾ cup grated Parmesan cheese
¼ cup milk	

(Timballo di Fettuccine)   **Serves 4 to 6**

6 tablespoons olive oil	pinch bicarbonate of soda
1 clove garlic, crushed	½ cup cold water
1 cup (1 ounce) Italian dried mush-	4 eggs
rooms, soaked in warm water 30	2 cups Béchamel sauce
minutes, squeezed dry	(page 212)
½ cup stock	½ pound ham, diced
1 pound medium egg noodles	¾ cup grated Parmesan cheese

Dice half of the meat; grind the rest with the celery, carrot and onion. Heat the oil and butter in a saucepan and brown the meat and vegetables lightly. Season with salt and pepper and add the wine. Reduce and add the tomatoes. Simmer until the meat is cooked and the sauce is thick. **To prepare the filling:** Mix the ricotta in a bowl with salt, pepper, nutmeg and milk; set aside. Cook the lasagne in plenty of boiling salted water. When done, remove with a slotted spoon and lay them out on a napkin to dry. Cut in rectangular pieces and arrange on a heat-resistant serving dish in layers, spreading each layer with some meat sauce and cheese. Pour the melted butter over the last layer and bake in preheated 450° F. oven for 10 minutes. Serve accompanied with grated Parmesan cheese.

Heat the oil in a large saucepan and brown the garlic lightly. Cut the mushrooms into small pieces and sauté lightly with the garlic. When the mushrooms are browned, add the stock, cover and simmer slowly. Cook the noodles in plenty of boiling salted water and soda until they are *al dente* (firm to the bite). Before draining, add the cold water. This will make the pasta light and separated. Beat the eggs in a large bowl, add the pasta, half the Béchamel sauce and the diced ham and mix well. Grease an 8-cup ring mold with butter, sprinkle it with the grated cheese and fill it with the pasta mixture. Cover the top layer of pasta with the remainder of the Béchamel sauce. Bake in a preheated 450° F. oven for 10 minutes. Invert the mold on a round hot serving dish and allow the noodles to settle before lifting it off. Serve with the mushroom sauce in the center of the ring.

NOODLES WITH ARTICHOKES

NOODLES WITH HARE

Photo Barilla

(Tagliolini ai Carciofi)   **Serves 4 to 6**

¼ cup olive oil
4 tablespoons butter
¼ onion
1 package (10 ounces) frozen artichoke
   hearts, defrosted

salt and freshly ground pepper
1 pound narrow egg noodles
3 eggs
¾ cup grated Parmesan cheese

(Pappardelle alla Lepre)   **Serves 4 to 6**

½ hare (about 2 pounds)
½ cup olive oil
7 tablespoons butter
1 stalk celery, chopped
1 onion, chopped
1 carrot, chopped
   salt and pepper
1 bay leaf

2 tablespoons flour
2 cups dry red wine
1 pound wide noodles
   pinch bicarbonate of soda
½ cup cold water
¼ cup melted butter
1 cup grated Parmesan cheese

Heat the oil and butter in a saucepan and sauté the onion until golden brown; discard it. Add the artichoke hearts and brown. When they are nearly cooked, add a little water, leaving the pot uncovered and the heat low. Season with salt and freshly ground pepper. Cook the noodles in plenty of boiling salted water. Beat the eggs with a few tablespoons of the grated cheese. When the noodles are *al dente* (firm to the bite), drain and add to the beaten eggs with the artichoke sauce and the rest of the cheese. Toss and turn into a warm oven-proof dish. Serve accompanied with additional grated Parmesan cheese.

Wash the hare well, remove any sinews and cut into pieces. Heat the oil and butter in a saucepan. Add the chopped vegetables, hare, salt, pepper and bay leaf. Sauté over high heat to remove excess moisture from the meat and to brown it. When it is beginning to brown, sprinkle with the flour. Add the wine and as soon as it begins to boil, cover the saucepan and reduce the heat to moderate. Simmer for about 2 hours or until meat is tender. Remove the bones and return the pieces of meat to the saucepan with the sauce and continue cooking for a short time. Cook the noodles in plenty of boiling salted water. Put a pinch bicarbonate of soda and the cold water into the saucepan before draining the pasta to keep it separated and light. Toss with the melted butter and grated Parmesan cheese. Arrange on a serving dish, placing the pieces of hare and the sauce over the pasta.

(Pappardelle al Cinghiale)   Serves 6

⅓ pound button mushrooms	½ cup red wine
1 onion	¼ cup grappa
1 carrot	1 recipe fresh egg pasta (page 46)
¾ pound smoked ham	pinch bicarbonate of soda
6 tablespoons lard	½ cup cold water
¼ cup olive oil	4 tablespoons melted butter
7 tablespoons butter	1 cup grated Parmesan cheese
salt and pepper	

Wipe the mushrooms with a damp cloth and slice finely. Put the onion, carrot, smoked ham and lard through a grinder. Cook this mixture gently in a saucepan with the olive oil and butter. Add the sliced mushrooms, salt and pepper; cook over high heat until the mushrooms are browned. Add the wine and grappa. When the liquid has evaporated, cover the saucepan, reduce the heat and cook the sauce slowly. Cut the pasta dough into strips 1⅛ to 1¼ inches wide and boil in plenty of salted water. Before draining the pasta, add the bicarbonate of soda and cold water. This will prevent the pasta from sticking together. Turn out onto a serving dish and pour the melted butter and a few tablespoons of the grated cheese over the pasta. Mix well with two wooden forks, lifting the pasta to coat it with the butter and cheese. Then add the smoked ham sauce. Serve accompanied with the remaining grated Parmesan cheese.

(Tortellini alla Panna con Tartufi)   Serves 8 to 9

¼ cup olive oil	⅔ cup grated Parmesan cheese
¼ pound lean veal, chopped	grated nutmeg
¼ pound pork, chopped	4¼ cups flour
¼ pound prosciutto, chopped	1 tablespoon butter
1 clove garlic	5 tablespoons melted butter
sprig rosemary	1 cup heavy cream
salt and pepper	3 egg yolks
½ cup dry white wine	3½ ounces white truffles, sliced
6 eggs	

To prepare the filling: Heat the oil in a saucepan and brown the chopped veal, pork and fatty part of ham with the garlic, rosemary, salt and pepper. Add wine and reduce. Cover and cook meat slowly. Discard garlic and rosemary and grind cooked meat with lean part of ham. Bind mixture with 1 egg, the cheese and a sprinkling of nutmeg. **To prepare the pasta:** Measure flour, with a pinch salt, onto a pastry board with a well in the center. Break 5 eggs into well and work into flour to form dough. Knead for 5 minutes. Let rest covered for 5 minutes. Roll out paper thin and cut into 2-inch circles. Put a little of the tortellini in the center of each circle, fold over, and press together. With the seam on the outside, curve and press to form a ring. Cook in plenty of boiling salted water with 1 tablespoon of butter until *al dente*. Remove with a slotted spoon to a saucepan. Add 4 tablespoons of melted butter and cream to the saucepan. Heat, mixing. Remove from heat and thicken with egg yolks and additional cheese. Serve on a heated platter, sprinkled with truffles. Pour remaining melted butter over the truffles and sprinkle with additional cheese. Put the dish into a preheated 450° F. oven for a few minutes; serve immediately.

STUFFED CORNETS WITH MEAT SAUCE

RAVIOLI WITH MUSHROOMS

(Tortellini al Sugo di Carne) **Serves 8 to 9**

6 tablespoons butter	1 cup dry red wine
¼ cup olive oil	2 tablespoons tomato paste
1 onion, finely chopped	2 quarts stock or water
1 carrot, finely chopped	¼ pound ham, chopped
1 stalk celery, finely chopped	¼ pound mortadella, chopped
¼ pound pork, diced	1¾ pounds tortellini with meat
¼ pound beef, diced	stuffing
salt and pepper	grated Parmesan cheese

(Ravioli ai Funghi) **Serves 4 to 6**

1 pound spinach	½ pound boiled ham, minced
1 tablespoon butter	1 cup grated Parmesan cheese
4¼ cups flour	salt
8 eggs	6 tablespoons melted butter
1¼ cups ricotta or cottage cheese	mushroom sauce (page 36)

Heat 4 tablespoons of the butter and oil in a saucepan and sauté the vegetables until they are browned. Add the pork and beef dice. Brown lightly, mixing well with the vegetables, and season with salt and pepper. Add the wine and reduce. Add the tomato paste, diluted with a little of the stock. Cover and simmer over low heat for about 30 minutes. Before removing the saucepan from the heat, stir the ham and mortadella into the sauce. Boil the tortellini in the remainder of the stock until they are al dente (firm to the bite). Remove with a slotted spoon into a deep, round serving dish. Pour the meat sauce over the tortellini and add the 2 tablespoons of butter. Serve very hot accompanied with grated Parmesan cheese. This dish, from the province of Emilia, should be served with red wine.

Steam the spinach, drain and put through a food mill. Place in a bowl or oven-proof dish. Add 1 tablespoon of the butter and place the dish in a warm oven to dry out the spinach. The oven should not be turned on. Make the pasta dough with the flour, 5 eggs, a pinch salt, and the spinach purée, working the purée in with the eggs following the directions on page 46. Knead and let rest for 30 minutes; roll out paper thin. Mix the ingredients together and roll out the dough. Cut the dough into 2½-inch squares. Prepare the filling by mixing the ricotta cheese with 3 eggs, the ham, ¾ cup of the grated Parmesan cheese and salt. Put a generous teaspoon of the filling on each of half of the squares. Cover with the remaining pasta squares, pressing the edges of the dough firmly together to seal tightly. Cook the ravioli in plenty of boiling salted water until al dente (firm to the bite); drain well. Mix gently with melted butter and a few spoonfuls of grated Parmesan cheese; arrange on a hot stainless steel oval dish. Cover the ravioli with the fresh mushroom sauce and serve accompanied with additional grated Parmesan cheese.

VERMICELLI WITH TURIDDU SAUCE

CHARCOAL BURNER'S SPAGHETTI

Photo Barilla

(Vermicelli alla Turiddu) **Serves 4 to 6**

½ cup olive oil
1 pound tomatoes, peeled, seeded and
    drained
10 to 15 pitted black olives
½ red pepper, chopped

salt
1 pound vermicelli
    dash olive oil
½ cup grated Parmesan cheese
    pinch oregano

(Bucatini alla Carbonara) **Serves 4 to 6**

1 pound large spaghetti (bucatini)
½ cup olive oil
1 clove garlic
½ pound pork, diced
5 eggs

salt
6 tablespoons grated Romano cheese
    freshly ground black pepper
6 tablespoons grated Parmesan
    cheese

Heat the ½ cup olive oil in a saucepan. Add the tomatoes, the whole olives and the red pepper; season with salt. Simmer until the sauce thickens. Cook the vermicelli in plenty of boiling salted water until it is *al dente* (firm to the bite). Drain and toss in a bowl with a dash olive oil, the grated Parmesan cheese and a pinch oregano. Arrange on a serving dish and pour the piping hot Turiddu over the vermicelli.

Prepare this authentic sauce, which the charcoal burners used to make over wood fires, while the pasta is cooking in plenty of boiling salted water. Heat the oil in a large saucepan and sauté the garlic until golden brown; add the diced pork. Beat the eggs in a bowl with a little salt, the grated Romano cheese and some freshly ground black pepper. When the spaghetti is *al dente* (firm to the bite), drain and add to the pork. Mix well, then remove the saucepan from the heat. Add the beaten eggs slowly, stirring constantly. Bring the piping hot *bucatini* to the table on a serving dish accompanied with grated Parmesan cheese.

SPIRAL MACARONI, ITALIAN STYLE

MACARONI WITH FONDUE SAUCE

Photo Barilla

Photo Barilla

(Tortiglioni all'Italiana)   **Serves 4 to 6**

1 pound spiral macaroni
2 tablespoons olive oil
1 or 2 tomatoes, peeled and cut in strips
½ clove garlic
¼ teaspoon basil
⅓ cup melted butter

½ cup grated Parmesan cheese
2 mozzarella cheeses, diced
   pepper
12 pitted black olives, coarsely
   chopped
2 teaspoons ground oregano

(Tortiglioni con Fonduta)   **Serves 4 to 6**

½ pound Fontina cheese, sliced
2 cups milk
4 egg yolks
   freshly grated white pepper

1 pound spiral macaroni
⅓ cup melted butter
¾ cup grated Parmesan cheese
2 ounces sliced white truffles

Cook the macaroni in plenty of boiling salted water. While it is cooking, heat the oil in a saucepan and sauté the tomato strips with the garlic and basil. When the macaroni is *al dente* (firm to the bite), drain and turn into a round oven-proof dish. Toss with the melted butter, grated Parmesan cheese, the cubed mozzarella cheese, pepper and the chopped olives. Add the oregano and few drops of garlic squeezed from a garlic press. Garnish with the strips of tomato in the sauce.

Cover the sliced Fontina cheese with 1 cup milk and soak for several hours. Put the cheese and milk into the top of a double boiler and cook over boiling water, beating constantly with a rotary beater, until the cheese has melted. Remove from heat. Beat 1 cup warm milk with the egg yolks. Add them to the melted cheese gradually, mixing thoroughly. Season with freshly grated white pepper. Cook the macaroni in plenty of boiling salted water until it is *al dente* (firm to the bite). Drain and turn into a bowl, tossing with the butter and grated Parmesan cheese. Stir in the fondue sauce and turn onto a hot serving dish. Garnish with the sliced white truffles.

GOURMET'S CANNELLONI

(Cannelloni del Gastronomo)　　　　　　　　**Serves 6**

½ cup olive oil
1 onion, chopped
½ pound lean veal, cut in small pieces
½ pound pork, cut in small pieces
½ pound Italian sausage, cut in small pieces
1 sprig rosemary
　salt
½ cup dry white wine

½ cup stock
½ pound veal sweetbreads, cut in small pieces
2 eggs
　pinch nutmeg
1 cup grated Parmesan cheese
1 recipe fresh egg pasta (page 46)
½ recipe Béchamel sauce (page 212)

To prepare the filling: Heat the oil in a skillet and sauté the onion until browned. Discard the onion and add the veal, pork and sausage with the rosemary; sauté until meat is browned. Season with salt and add the wine. When the wine has evaporated, add stock and transfer the meat to a preheated 350° F. oven to continue cooking until dry. Add the sweetbreads to the meat shortly before taking it from the oven. Discard the rosemary and put all the meats through a grinder. Add the eggs, nutmeg and grated Parmesan cheese to this mixture. Roll the pasta dough wafer thin and cut into 4×6-inch rectangles; dry for 1 hour. Cook the pasta in plenty of boiling salted water for 4 minutes; remove with a slotted spoon and plunge into cold water. Lay the cooked pasta rectangles on a clean damp cloth. Cover each bit of pasta with a layer of filling. Roll up the rectangles into tubes, closing the edges by pressing together with the fingers. Cover the bottom of an oven-proof gratin dish with a layer of Béchamel sauce. Put the cannelloni in the dish in rows and cover them with the remainder of the Béchamel sauce. Sprinkle additional Parmesan cheese over the top and put the dish in a preheated 350° F. oven for 15 minutes. Serve immediately.

MACARONI, GYPSY STYLE

Photo Barilla

(Mezze Maniche alla Zingara)　　　　**Serves 4 to 6**

1 pound macaroni
6 ripe tomatoes, peeled, seeded and chopped
¼ cup olive oil
1 clove garlic

1 red pepper, chopped
10 pitted black olives, chopped
　oregano
　salt

Cook the macaroni in plenty of boiling salted water. While it is cooking prepare the sauce. Drain the chopped tomatoes. Heat the oil in a saucepan and sauté the garlic and pepper. Add the drained tomatoes, chopped olives, oregano and salt. Cook the sauce until it thickens and the flavors have mingled. As soon as the pasta is drained, serve it with this many-flavored sauce.

Rice, introduced into Italy in the fifteenth century by the Spaniards, is used as a first course. In many regions of northern Italy it even competes with the pasta. Originally the only seasoning used was salt. Gradually, however, the more sophisticated recipes of some modern rice dishes were achieved by using more varied flavorings. Almost every tourist area in Italy has its own particular way of serving rice. The dishes of the coastal regions are made with seafood or fish, the inland areas preferring those made with mushrooms, truffles or game. The traditional regional dishes are sometimes adapted according to the personal variations of the chefs.

At one time there was a subtle distinction between rice dishes and risotto dishes. Rice dishes were those cooked in water and seasoned afterward with a sauce while risotto dishes were cooked in a fatty broth with the seasonings, oil and butter added at the outset. This distinction no longer exists. Rice salads are always popular. They are served cold and are appealing, colorful and imaginative, ranging from the bright red of tomatoes to the vivid green of peppers.

RICE SALAD MONTGLAS

SHRIMP RISOTTO

Photo Curtiriso

(Insalata di Riso alla Montglas)　　　　　**Serves 6**

    2 cups rice
   10 ounces smoked tongue
   10 ounces boiled ham
    5 tablespoons butter
  1¾ ounces goose liver pâté
   ¼ cup marsala
      salt
      pepper
      pinch of nutmeg
   ½ cup heavy cream
    4 hard cooked eggs, cut into
      rounds and wedges
   ½ pound boiled chicken, flaked
    2 small black truffles, sliced
      pinch saffron

(Risotto di Gamberetti)　　　　　**Serves 6**

  1¼ pounds shrimp
   ¼ cup olive oil
   ¼ onion, chopped
    2 cloves garlic, chopped
      salt and pepper
    1 cup dry white wine
   ¼ cup brandy
    4 tablespoons butter
    2 cups rice
    1 quart hot fish stock or bottled
      clam juice
    2 tablespoons olive oil

Boil the rice in plenty of salted water; remove it from the heat when it is still firm but cooked. Drain and rinse it under running cold water; drain once more. Put it into a dish to dry, separating the grains with a fork. Cut out about 12 ⅛-inch-thick rounds about 2¼ inches in diameter from the tongue and ham. Grind the remainder of the tongue and ham; cream the butter until light and fluffy. Mix them with the goose liver pâté. Moisten the mixture with the marsala and season with a little salt, pepper and nutmeg. Spread the filling lightly on the rounds of meat and sandwich together a round of ham with a round of tongue. Put these rounds in the refrigerator to stiffen. Toss the cold rice with the cream, hard cooked eggs, chicken and sliced truffles. Give the mixture a touch of color by adding a little saffron diluted in a little water. Arrange the rice on a serving dish in a dome shape, surround it with the stuffed rounds of meat and decorate the center with piped creamed butter shaped in the form of a flower.

Rinse the shrimp several times in water and shell them. Heat the ¼ cup oil in a saucepan and sauté the onion and garlic until lightly browned. Add the shrimp and cook gently; season with salt and pepper. Add the wine and brandy and simmer the sauce for about 10 minutes. Set aside a few shrimp to garnish the dish. Melt the butter in another saucepan, add the rice and let it absorb the butter, stirring constantly. As the rice gradually becomes dry, add alternately the hot fish stock and the shrimp sauce, a little at a time, letting the rice absorb the liquid between each addition. When the rice is cooked, add the 2 tablespoons olive oil; the risotto should be clear and soft. Turn it into a hot oven-proof dish and serve garnished with the reserved shrimp.

RICE WITH LARGE CRAYFISH

Photo Curtiriso

(Risotto di Gamberoni) **Serves 6**

1 pound crayfish
2 teaspoons salt
¼ cup vinegar
   juice of ½ lemon
¼ cup olive oil

2 cups rice
1 clove garlic
2 tablespoons olive oil
   chopped parsley
   parsley sprigs

Wash and clean the crayfish carefully, splitting the shell down the back and removing the intestine with a knife. Boil them in their shells in 5 cups of water with the salt, vinegar and lemon juice. Shell them and keep hot in the water in which they were cooked. Heat the ¼ cup olive oil in a saucepan and lightly cook the rice; flavor it with a few drops of garlic from a garlic press. Pour on top of the rice enough of the hot crayfish stock (about 1 quart) to be absorbed during cooking. Add most of the crayfish to the rice, reserving a few for garnish. Cook the risotto over medium heat in a covered saucepan, but do not stir it. On taking it from the heat, add the 2 tablespoons olive oil; toss the grains of rice with a fork to separate and add the chopped parsley. Arrange on a serving dish and decorate with the reserved crayfish and parsley sprigs.

RICE WITH FROG LEGS AND CRAYFISH

Photo Curtiriso

(Riso con Rane e Gamberi) **Serves 6**

1 pound frog legs
1 pound crayfish
2 teaspoons salt
1 tablespoon vinegar
½ cup dry white wine
2 stalks fennel
1 stalk celery
3½ tablespoons butter
2 cups soft bread crumbs
½ cup light cream
1⅓ cups grated Mascarpone cheese

1 tablespoon grated Parmesan
   cheese
2 eggs
2 egg yolks
   pinch cinnamon
3 tablespoons flour
   olive oil
2 cups rice
½ onion, chopped
   lemon slices
   parsley sprigs

Clean the frog legs and skin. Shell the crayfish and rinse well under running water. Cook the frog legs and crayfish in a saucepan in 5 cups boiling water with the 2 teaspoons salt, vinegar, wine, fennel and celery for 5 minutes or until tender. Remove the frog legs and crayfish and strain the stock. Chop the meat from the frog legs and crayfish finely and brown lightly (reserving a few of the crayfish for garnish) in a saucepan with 1½ tablespoons of the butter; cool. Soak the bread crumbs in the cream and mix with the browned meat, Mascarpone cheese, Parmesan cheese, 1 whole egg and 2 egg yolks. Season with salt and a pinch cinnamon and shape the mixture into little round rissoles. Dredge in flour, dip them in a beaten egg and fry in hot oil. Sauté the rice in the remaining butter with the onion, then add 1 quart of the strained stock. Cook until the rice has absorbed the stock. Mold the rice into a domed shape in a bowl and turn out onto a round serving dish. Place the rissoles, a few whole crayfish, lemon slices and parsley sprigs around the rice.

(Risotto con Vongole)   Serves 6

3¼ pounds clams
¼ cup olive oil
2 cloves garlic, chopped
½ cup dry white wine
2 tablespoons brandy

salt and pepper
5 tablespoons butter
2 cups rice
chopped parsley
2 tablespoons olive oil

(Riso con San Daniele)   Serves 6

⅓ cup olive oil
½ onion, chopped
¾ to 1 pound brown mushrooms,
sliced
2 cups rice
1 quart hot clear stock
7 tablespoons butter

1 cup grated Parmesan cheese
chopped parsley
salt
¼ pound prosciutto, sliced
1 package (10 ounces) cooked
frozen peas

Scrub the clams carefully under running water. Put ½ cup water in a saucepan over high heat, adding the clams to allow them to open. Remove the flesh as the shells open. Strain the stock in the saucepan and keep it hot on the stove. Heat the ¼ cup oil in another saucepan and sauté the garlic until it is golden brown. Add the clams and simmer gently, then pour in the wine and brandy and season with salt and pepper. Cover the saucepan and simmer the clams in their own steam. If necessary, add a little of the stock obtained when opening the clams. Heat the butter in a skillet, add the rice and let it absorb the butter, stirring constantly. Add the stock from the clams, stirring until the mixture reaches the boiling point. Reduce the heat to medium. Add the clams with their sauce and simmer until the risotto is still firm but cooked, adding extra water when necessary. When the rice is ready, correct seasoning and add the chopped parsley and the 2 tablespoons of olive oil. Serve the risotto in a warm oven-proof dish.

Heat the oil in a saucepan and sauté the onion. Add the mushrooms and brown, then add the rice. When the rice has absorbed the oil, add the hot stock gradually, stirring continuously. Remove the rice from the heat as soon as it is still firm but cooked and toss it with the butter, ½ cup of the grated Parmesan cheese and the chopped parsley. Add salt to taste. Grease a round oven-proof mold dish with butter, pack it with the risotto and place it in a pan in about 1 inch of water in a preheated 350° F. oven for 30 minutes. Let it stand a few minutes before turning it out onto a round warm serving dish. Garnish with slices of Prosciutto and surround with buttered green peas. Serve accompanied with the remaining grated Parmesan cheese.

SEAFOOD RISOTTO

CRABMEAT RISOTTO

(Risotto con Frutti di Mare)   Serves 6

¼ pound squid
¼ pound shrimp
¼ pound crayfish
1 pound mussels
1 pound clams
   bouquet garni
   salt
½ cup olive oil

1 clove garlic, crushed
1 green chili pepper, chopped
¼ cup dry white wine
¼ cup marsala
¼ pound scallops
2 cups rice
   chopped parsley

(Risotto con Polpa di Granchio)   Serves 6

1 to 1½ pounds crabmeat
½ cup olive oil
1 clove garlic
1 medium tomato, peeled
   and seeded
1 quart fish stock or bottled clam
   juice

4 tablespoons butter
2 cups rice
   salt and pepper
   chopped parsley

Cut out the eyes and mouth of the squid. Remove the ink sac and internal bone. Cut off the tough points on the tentacles. Rub off the skin and wash under running water until white. Shell the shrimp and crayfish. Put about ½ cup water in a saucepan over high heat and add the mussels and clams to open them. Remove the flesh from the shells and strain the liquid in the saucepan; return to the saucepan. Add enough extra water to the saucepan to make 1 quart and boil the squid, shrimp and crayfish with a bouquet garni and a little salt. This court bouillon will be used for cooking the rice later. Heat ¼ cup of the oil in a saucepan with the crushed garlic and sauté all of the fish. Season with salt and chopped chili pepper, then add the wine and marsala. When the wines have reduced, add a few tablespoons of the court bouillon and leave the saucepan uncovered on low heat to simmer, adding the scallops about 5 minutes before serving. Heat the remaining ¼ cup oil in a saucepan and cook the rice lightly. Add the court bouillon gradually, stirring constantly, and boil the rice until it is still firm but cooked. Remove from the heat and turn it into a hot dish. Garnish with the seafood, cover with sauce and sprinkle with parsley and a few tablespoons of olive oil.

Pick over the crabmeat and remove any cartilage. Heat the oil in a saucepan and sauté the garlic. Add the tomatoes and cook over high heat, stirring, until the sauce has thickened. Reduce the heat and add the crabmeat, reserving a few pieces for garnish. Heat the fish stock. Melt the butter in a saucepan and sauté the rice until it has absorbed all the butter. Add the hot fish stock. Cook over high heat without stirring. After about 10 minutes stir the crabmeat and the sauce into the rice, adding more stock if necessary. Season with salt and pepper to taste. When the rice is still firm but cooked, turn it out on a serving dish. Garnish with the reserved crabmeat and sprinkle with a dash olive oil and some chopped parsley.

BLACK SQUID RISOTTO

RICE WITH RICOTTA CHEESE

Photo Curtiriso

(Risotto di Seppie Nere)   **Serves 6**

1½ pounds squid	1 green chili pepper, chopped
6 tablespoons olive oil	½ cup dry white wine
2 cloves garlic, chopped	2 cups rice
1 medium onion, chopped	chopped parsley
salt	

(Riso con Ricotta)   **Serves 6**

7 tablespoons butter	⅓ pound ground veal
2¼ pounds tomatoes, peeled	2 cups rice
1 onion, chopped	1¼ cups ricotta or cottage cheese
1 stalk celery, chopped	3 eggs, beaten
1 carrot, chopped	1 mozzarella cheese, diced
1 tablespoon chopped basil, or ½ teaspoon dried	pinch nutmeg
salt	7 tablespoons grated Parmesan cheese
2 tablespoons olive oil	1 tomato for garnish

Cut out the eyes and mouth of the squid. Remove the ink sac and internal bone. Cut off the tough points on the tentacles. Rub off the skin and wash under running water until white. Rinse three or four of the ink sacs very carefully and reserve. Slice the squid. Heat the oil in a saucepan and sauté the garlic and onion; add the squid and cook over high heat, adding salt, the chili pepper and the wine. When the wine has reduced, add the black liquid from the sacs which were kept aside. Cover, reduce the heat and simmer for about 30 minutes. Add the rice, stirring until it has absorbed the sauce. Continue cooking, adding small amounts of slightly salted boiling water when necessary, until the rice is still firm but cooked; let it stand for 1 minute off the heat. Add the chopped parsley and a dash olive oil. Turn into a hot oven-proof dish and serve.

Melt the butter in a saucepan and sauté the tomatoes, onion, celery, carrot and basil briefly. Purée through a vegetable mill and return the sauce to the heat until it thickens, seasoning with salt and oil. Prepare round rissoles from the ground veal and cook them in the tomato-flavored sauce. Boil the rice in plenty of salted water until it is still firm but cooked. Drain and toss with a fork. When it is cold, add the ricotta cheese, eggs, mozzarella, nutmeg, a little of the tomato sauce and the grated Parmesan cheese. Put the rice into a buttered oven-proof mold and place it in a preheated 450° F. oven for 5 minutes; turn out onto a round serving dish. Put the rissoles around and on top of the rice; and cover with remaining sauce.

RICE, EASTERN STYLE

(Riso all'Orientale) **Serves 6**

6 cups clear stock	½ pound Italian sausage, sliced
2 cups rice	2 eggs
8 tablespoons butter	salt
1 onion, chopped	2 tablespoons grated Parmesan
1 green chili pepper, chopped	cheese
¼ pound lean pork, sliced	½ cup cooked green peas
¼ pound boiled chicken,	
finely chopped	

Heat the stock. Sauté the rice lightly with 2 tablespoons of the butter and half of the onion in an oven-proof casserole. Add the stock; it should cover the rice. When the stock comes to the boil, cover the casserole and put it into a preheated 400° F. oven for about 20 minutes or until all the liquid is absorbed and the rice is tender. Mix 2 tablespoons of butter and the chili pepper into the rice with a fork in order to separate the grains. Sauté the pork, chicken and sausage with the remaining onion and butter. Reduce the heat and simmer gently, adding a little stock. Make an omelette with the eggs, salt and the cheese. Roll it up and slice into fine strips; add to the meat sauce. Pour the sauce over the rice and mix well. Arrange the rice on a serving dish and garnish the edge of the dish with the green peas and some of the sliced sausage from the sauce.

RICE WITH ITALIAN SAUSAGE

(Riso con Salsiccia) **Serves 6**

⅔ cup cooked peas	2 red peppers, sliced
7 tablespoons butter	salt and pepper
1 onion, chopped	6 cups clear stock
¼ cup olive oil	2 cups rice
½ pound Italian sausage,	¾ cup grated Parmesan cheese
cut in chunks	

Simmer the peas in 2 tablespoons of the butter. Sauté a little of the onion in the oil in a small saucepan. Add the Italian sausage, the red pepper and the peas and then cook gently. Season with salt and pepper. Simmer this sauce gently while preparing the risotto. Heat the stock. Put 2 tablespoons of the butter in a pan with the remainder of the onion. When the onion is limp but still not browned, stir in the rice and let it absorb the onion flavor. When the rice begins to crackle, spread it over the bottom of the pan with a wooden spoon and cover it with the hot stock. Do not stir. Cover and place the rice and stock in a preheated 350° F. for about 25 minutes. When the rice is thoroughly cooked, it will have absorbed all the stock. Remove the dish from the oven and add the remaining butter, tossing the rice with a fork to separate the grains and make them shiny. Arrange the rice in a well-heated deep dish and cover it with the vegetable and sausage sauce. Serve accompanied with grated Parmesan cheese.

EGG RISOTTO

RICE WITH CURRIED SOLE

(Risotto all'Uovo)   **Serves 6**

1 quart clear stock
8 tablespoons butter
2 cups rice
5 egg yolks

½ cup cream
¾ cup grated Parmesan cheese
   pinch nutmeg
   salt

(Riso all'Indiana)   **Serves 6**

2 cups rice
1 onion, chopped
1 green apple, chopped
½ cup clarified butter
1 tablespoon curry powder
   salt

1 cup heavy cream
12 small sole fillets
   lemon juice
3 tablespoons flour
2 tablespoons butter

Keep the stock hot on the stove. Melt half of the butter in a skillet, add the rice and let it absorb the butter. Add a ladleful of stock and cook the rice over a high heat, adding additional stock as the rice becomes dry. When the rice is cooked, add the rest of the butter to give it a shiny texture. Beat the egg yolks with the cream, and add the Parmesan cheese, nutmeg and salt. Remove the skillet from the stove, keeping the rice hot, and add the creamy egg mixture slowly and carefully. Let the risotto stand for a few minutes, then serve it in warm soup plates accompanied with additional grated Parmesan cheese.

Boil the rice, stirring occasionally, in a large saucepan of salted water until it is cooked but still firm. Drain and cool under running cold water. Drain once more and spread the rice on a baking sheet covered with a dish towel. Cover with a second towel and place in a warm oven for a few minutes to dry out. The grains of rice will then be hot and well separated. Sauté the onion and apple gently in a skillet in the clarified butter. Dilute the curry powder with a little water and add it to the skillet. Season the sauce with salt, add the cream and simmer for 10 minutes till the flavors are well mingled. Wash the sole fillets well in water and lemon juice and dry them with paper towels. Flatten each fillet with the palm of the hand, dip in flour and sauté in the 2 tablespoons of butter until golden brown, adding more butter if needed. Take the rice from the oven and arrange it on a hot serving dish. Roll the fillets, place them on top of the rice and cover with the curry sauce. Serve immediately.

RISOTTO A LA MILANESE

APULIAN RICE

(Risotto alla Milanese)   **Serves 6**

1 quart stock	½ cup dry white wine
12 tablespoons butter	1½ ounces saffron filaments
3 tablespoons beef marrow, finely chopped	¾ cup grated Parmesan cheese
½ onion, finely chopped	salt
2 cups rice	freshly ground pepper

("Tiella" di Riso alla Pugliese)   **Serves 6 to 8**

1 pound clams or mussels	salt
¼ cup olive oil	2 cups rice
1 clove garlic, chopped	1½ quarts clear fish stock
1 pound fresh sardines	2 eggs, beaten
2 onions, sliced	4 tablespoons tomato purée
2 tomatoes, peeled and sliced	1 green pepper, cut in strips
3 potatoes, sliced	black olives
1 tablespoon saffron	parsley sprig

Heat the stock and keep it hot. Melt 4 tablespoons of the butter in a saucepan and sauté the marrow and the chopped onion gently, not allowing the onion to brown. Add the rice and sauté for a few minutes, stirring constantly with a wooden spoon. Increase the heat to high and add the hot stock gradually as the rice swells and becomes dry, stirring all the time. After 10 minutes, pour in the white wine with some more stock. Soak the saffron in a little hot stock. A few minutes before removing the rice from the heat add the strained stock in which the saffron was soaked. The saffron liquid is added at the end of the cooking time so that the flavor is more pronounced. Add the rest of the butter and ¼ cup of the grated Parmesan cheese to the risotto. Stir in a little salt, if necessary, and some freshly ground pepper. Serve the risotto in hot earthenware dishes accompanied with the remaining grated Parmesan cheese.

Wash the clams in running water and brush the shells well. (If using mussels, wash, scrub and "beard" them.) Heat a little of the oil in a skillet and cook the clams or mussels with the garlic over high heat until the shells open. Remove the flesh from the shells; strain the liquid in the skillet through a fine cloth and reserve. Scale, fillet and chop the sardines. Put a layer of sliced onions in a casserole and sprinkle with the remaining oil. Cook the onion lightly, then add the tomatoes, sardines and potatoes; cook for a short time with the reserved strained liquid. Dissolve the saffron in the liquid and season with salt. Cover and simmer gently over low heat. Add the rice and clams or mussels to the thickened sauce. Cover the rice with the fish stock and put the dish in a preheated 400° F. oven for about 15 to 18 minutes. When the rice is completely cooked, it will have absorbed all the stock but will still be moist because of the sauce. Remove from the oven and mix in the beaten eggs with a fork; add a dash of olive oil. Serve from the casserole, garnishing the top with some piped-on tomato purée, strips of green pepper, black olives and a parsley sprig.

RICE DIAMONDS WITH QUAILS	RICE MOLD

(Crostoni di Riso con Quaglie)   **Serves 6**

2 cups rice	2 eggs, beaten
2 quarts clear stock	6 quails, boned (with legs intact)
½ pound butter	¼ teaspoon sage
¾ cup grated Parmesan cheese	1 roast chicken, boned
pinch nutmeg	1 roll soaked in milk
½ cup milk	bread crumbs
4 egg yolks	½ cup dry red wine

(Bomba alla Parmigiana)   **Serves 6**

3 squabs	½ pound sausage
¼ pound salt pork, sliced	4 tablespoons butter
½ cup olive oil	2 cups rice
1 cup dry white wine	1 quart hot stock
salt and pepper	pitted green Spanish olives
1 onion, chopped,	parsley
3 squab livers, chopped	

Boil the rice in the stock. Drain and mix with 6 tablespoons of the butter, Parmesan cheese, nutmeg and milk. When it is cold, bind the rice mixture with two egg yolks. Roll ⅜ inch thick on a marble table. Cut into diamond-shaped pieces, dip in beaten eggs and sauté in some of the butter. When cooked, keep them hot at the side of the stove. Sauté the quails in a saucepan with 6 tablespoons of the butter and the sage. Reserve the sauce and quail legs; grind the quail and chicken meat with the roll soaked in milk. Add two egg yolks to this ground mixture and shape it into six croquettes. Dip them in beaten eggs, then in bread crumbs and fry in remaining butter. Put the sauce in which the quails were sautéed in a small saucepan and add the wine. Boil until the sauce is concentrated and the quantity reduced by half. Arrange the fried rice diamonds on a serving dish. Put a croquette on each one, placing quail leg on either side of the croquette to give the appearance of a whole quail. Sprinkle with the sauce and heat the dish in a preheated 350° F. oven before bringing it to the table.

Cover the breasts of the squabs with slices of salt pork, tying them on to keep them in place. Brown the squabs in olive oil in a saucepan. Pour in ½ cup of the wine and season with salt and pepper. Cover and simmer slowly for 30 minutes or until the squabs are tender. Bone two of the squabs but leave the third one whole. Set aside and warm. Heat the butter in a saucepan and sauté the onion, livers and sausage. Add the remaining wine and when it has evaporated, cover the saucepan. Simmer the sauce for 30 minutes and then add the rice. Stir, and when the rice has absorbed all the sauce, pour in the hot stock a little at a time until the rice is cooked but still firm. Toss the rice with the sauce and place it in a round greased mold. Put the mold into a hot oven for a few minutes. Turn out onto a white porcelain serving dish. Garnish the base of the mold with the pieces of squab and place the whole squab on the top, holding it in place with a skewer.

RICE AND BEAN SOUP

RISOTTO WITH BEANS

Photo Curtiriso

(Minestra di Riso e Fagioli)   Serves 6

1¼ cups dried pea beans	1 green chili pepper, chopped
salt	4 tomatoes, sliced
½ onion, chopped	6 tablespoons olive oil
½ carrot, chopped	2 cups rice
1 stalk celery, chopped	¾ cup grated Parmesan cheese

(Risotto con Fagioli)   Serves 6

½ cup olive oil	1 teaspoon tomato purée
1 onion, chopped	1 quart clear stock
3 cups shelled fava beans	salt
10 tablespoons butter	2 cups rice
2 tablespoons flour	¾ cup grated Parmesan cheese
2 cups mellow red wine	

Soak the beans overnight. The next day, drain them and put them in a saucepan with sufficient water to cover. Cover the saucepan and bring the water to a boil. Reduce the heat and simmer for 1½ to 2 hours. When the beans are tender, remove from the heat and season with salt to taste. Set aside. Sauté the chopped vegetables, and sliced tomatoes in olive oil in a large saucepan. Drain the beans, reserving the liquor, and add them to the vegetables. Simmer the beans and vegetables together, allowing the flavors to blend. Add the reserved bean liquor and bring to a boil. Add the rice. Cook for 15 to 18 minutes, stirring constantly, adding more liquid if necessary. When the rice is cooked, serve the soup accompanied with grated Parmesan cheese.

Heat the olive oil in a deep saucepan and sauté the onion until golden brown. Add the fava beans; simmer lightly. Knead together 2 tablespoons of the butter and the flour and add to the saucepan. Pour in the wine, let it evaporate and add the tomato purée diluted in a little stock. Cover and simmer over low heat until the beans are cooked. Add salt to taste. Sauté the rice in 4 tablespoons of the butter in a saucepan. Add the remaining stock gradually until the rice is cooked. Shortly before removing the rice from the heat, stir in half of the bean sauce and the remaining butter to give the rice a shiny appearance. Serve the risotto in soup plates, with the beans and sauce in the center of each dish. Accompany with grated Parmesan cheese.

RISOTTO WITH MUSHROOMS

RISOTTO WITH ASPARAGUS

(Risotto con Funghi)   **Serves 6**

2 cloves garlic (inner buds removed), sliced	2 tablespoons chopped parsley
½ cup olive oil	3½ tablespoons butter
¾ pound mushrooms, finely chopped	2 cups rice
salt	1 quart hot clear stock
	¾ cup grated Parmesan cheese

(Risotto con Asparagi)   **Serves 6**

4 tablespoons butter	5 tablespoons grated Parmesan cheese
¼ onion, chopped	salt and pepper
2 cups rice	pinch nutmeg
1 quart hot clear stock	4 eggs, beaten
2 pounds asparagus	
¾ cup heavy cream	

Sauté the garlic slices in olive oil, add the mushrooms and cook quickly over high heat. Remove the pan from the heat, add salt and the chopped parsley. Set aside and keep warm. Melt 2 tablespoons of the butter in a saucepan and sauté the rice, stirring until it has absorbed the butter. Add the hot stock gradually, stirring constantly. After 10 minutes, add some of the mushrooms with their sauce. When the rice is swollen and soft, add the remaining butter to give it a shiny appearance. Season with salt to taste and add a few table-spoons grated Parmesan cheese. Serve the risotto in soup plates with some of the mushrooms and sauce in the center of each plate. Accompany with remaining grated Parmesan cheese.

Heat 2 tablespoons of the butter in a saucepan and sauté the onion lightly until golden brown. Add the rice and sauté, stirring constantly. Add the hot stock gradually and continue to stir until the rice is cooked but still firm. Before removing the rice from the heat, stir in the remaining butter to give the rice a shiny appearance. Turn it into an oval oven-proof dish. Wash and clean the asparagus and toss the spears gently in a skillet with some additional butter. When they are almost cooked, arrange them in rows on top of the rice. Mix the cream, Parmesan cheese, salt, pepper, and the nutmeg with the eggs. Pour the sauce over the asparagus and sprinkle some additional grated Parmesan cheese over the top. Brown lightly in a preheated 450° F. oven and serve immediately.

(Risotto con Rognone)   Serves 6

2 veal kidneys
3 tablespoons flour
½ cup olive oil
1 clove garlic, crushed
  salt
  pepper
2 tablespoons chopped parsley

¼ cup dry marsala
6 tablespoons butter
¼ onion, finely chopped
2 cups rice
1 quart hot clear stock
¾ cup grated Parmesan cheese

(Risotto con Tartufi)   Serves 6

¼ onion, sliced
10 tablespoons butter
2 cups rice
1 quart hot clear stock

  salt
1 can (2 ounces) white or black
  truffles, thinly sliced
1 cup grated Parmesan cheese
2 tablespoons melted butter

Carefully clean the kidneys, removing any trace of fat. Soak them for 2 hours in cold salted water. Drain well and slice finely; dredge in flour. Heat the oil in a saucepan and sauté the garlic until golden. Add the kidneys and season with salt and pepper and the chopped parsley. Add the marsala and simmer over low heat. Heat 4 tablespoons of the butter in a saucepan and sauté the onion lightly. Add the rice. Pour the hot stock in gradually, stirring constantly, until the rice is cooked. Before removing the rice from the heat, stir in 2 tablespoons of butter to give it a shiny appearance. Butter a 6-cup ring mold well. Fill it lightly with the risotto; do not press it down. Place in a preheated 450° F. oven for a few minutes. Turn the risotto out into a deep serving dish and fill the center with the kidney sauce. Garnish with a little additional chopped parsley and serve accompanied with grated Parmesan cheese.

Sauté the onion in a saucepan with half of the butter. When the onion is golden brown, add the rice and cook gently until it has absorbed the butter. Add the hot stock gradually as the rice becomes dry, stirring constantly with a wooden spoon. Cook for 15 to 18 minutes or until the rice is tender; season with salt to taste. Stir in 4 tablespoons of the butter to give the rice a shiny appearance and turn it out on a hot oven-proof dish. Garnish with the truffles, sprinkle with the grated Parmesan cheese and finally pour 2 tablespoons of hot melted butter over the risotto.

GARDENER'S RICE MOLD

Photo Curtiriso

(Timballo di Riso all'Ortolana)   **Serves 6**

2 cups shelled peas	salt and pepper
clear stock	2 cups rice
3 tablespoons butter	2 eggplants, cut in strips
½ onion, chopped	3 zucchini, cut in strips
½ pound ground beef	⅔ cup olive oil
½ cup dry white wine	1 cup dry bread crumbs
1¼ pounds tomatoes, peeled	¾ cup grated Parmesan cheese
3 yellow peppers, sliced	

Cook the peas in clear stock, then toss them in 1 tablespoon of the butter. Sauté the onion in the remaining butter in a skillet without browning. Add the ground meat, wine, ¼ pound of the tomatoes and the peppers. Season with salt and pepper. Cover and simmer slowly until the sauce has thickened. Remove the slices of pepper and reserve. Boil the rice in plenty of salted water. Drain and toss with half of the sauce. Sauté the eggplants and zucchini in hot olive oil. Grease a rectangular baking dish and sprinkle it with bread crumbs. Put a layer of rice on the bottom of the baking dish and sprinkle with some of the grated Parmesan cheese. Cover with a layer of peas and some of the remaining tomatoes, cut in strips. Sprinkle with some more cheese and add a few tablespoons of the meat sauce. Cover this layer with more rice, the eggplant, grated cheese and meat sauce. Continue with another layer of rice and then a layer of eggplant, grated cheese and meat sauce. End with a layer of rice and dot with additional butter. Put into a preheated 450° F. oven for 5 minutes. Invert on a platter and serve surrounded by buttered green peas and garnished with the rest of the tomatoes, cut in strips, and the reserved pepper.

79

NEAPOLITAN RICE MOLD

Photo Curtiriso

(Timballo di Riso alla Napoletana)   **Serves 6**

2 cups rice	¼ pound Italian sausage, sliced
1 cup tomato purée	¼ cup olive oil
1½ quarts clear stock	½ pound chicken giblets
2 tablespoons butter	10 slices bread, torn into crumbs
¾ cup grated Parmesan cheese	1 cup milk
4 eggs, beaten	2 cups ground boiled beef
⅓ cup (⅓ ounce) Italian dried	flour
mushrooms, soaked in water	2 cups dry bread crumbs
30 minutes, squeezed dry	1 mozzarella cheese, cubed

Mix the rice with ¼ cup of the tomato purée and boil it in the stock until cooked but still firm. Remove from the heat and add the butter, Parmesan cheese and two beaten eggs. Cook the risotto, spreading it out in a wide saucepan and separating the grains of rice. Sauté the sausage gently in 2 tablespoons of the oil. Add the mushrooms to the sausage with the giblets and remaining tomato purée. Soak the bread crumbs in milk and mix with the ground beef. Shape into small, round rissoles, dredge in flour and brown them in the remaining oil. Add the rissoles to the mushroom and giblet sauce. Butter a round mold and cover the inside of it with the dry bread crumbs mixed with the remaining beaten eggs. Using a spoon, press about two-thirds of the rice around the sides leaving a well in the center. Fill it with the mushroom and giblet sauce (with the rissoles and giblets removed) and the cubed mozzarella cheese. Dot with butter and sprinkle with a generous tablespoon of grated Parmesan cheese. Cover with the remaining rice and put into a preheated 400° F. oven for 20 minutes. Remove from the oven and let stand for a few minutes before turning out. Serve it at once, surrounded by the rissoles and chicken giblets.

80

Soups

Soups are, in a sense, similar to cocktails: their ingredients are mixed together to provide a subtle blend of flavors which vary depending on the cooking time. The flavors which emerge are part of a precise tradition and it is easy to see similarities between towns and regions which suggest a common origin. The recipes gathered here embody the basic ideas and flavors which have evolved in cooking Italian soups over the centuries. They show that with careful preparation the flavors of even the poorest ingredients can be used to the best possible advantage. Many of the recipes, especially those where beans are used, date from the Middle Ages.

CHICKEN SOUP

MACARONI AND CHICK PEA SOUP

(Zuppa di Pollo)   **Serves 6**

2½ to 3 pounds whole chicken
    bouquet garni
    salt and pepper
  3 carrots, diced
  ½ celeriac, diced
  3 potatoes, diced
  ½ pound leeks, thinly sliced

  2 pounds peas, shelled, or 1
      package (10 ounces) frozen
      peas
1½ tablespoons butter
    toasted croutons
    grated Parmesan cheese

(Minestra di Pasta e Ceci)   **Serves 6**

½ pound dried chick peas
1 teaspoon bicarbonate of soda
½ teaspoon salt
  pepper
⅛ pound (generous) salt pork,
    blanched and cubed

1 clove garlic, chopped
¼ cup olive oil
2½ cups elbow macaroni
    grated Parmesan cheese

Clean and wash the chicken and put it in an earthenware or soup pot with just enough water to cover. Add the bouquet garni and salt and pepper to taste. Let the chicken boil slowly, skimming the liquid carefully to produce a clear, thin stock. When the chicken is tender (after about 1½ hours), take it out of the stock and cut into pieces, removing the bones but trying to keep the meat intact. Put the meat back in the stock and keep hot. Sauté all the vegetables (except the peas) lightly with a little butter in a saucepan. Add a little of the stock to the vegetables and simmer about 20 minutes until almost tender. Add the peas and simmer 10 minutes or until the peas are tender; when the vegetables are ready, pour them into the pot containing the chicken and stock and heat the soup for a few minutes. Serve very hot in little earthenware pots or soup bowls and accompanied with toasted croutons and grated Parmesan cheese.

Soak the chick peas for 24 hours in a bowl of cold water in which 1 teaspoon bicarbonate of soda has been dissolved. The following day, drain the peas and boil them slowly in 2 quarts of water for about 2 hours or until tender. When they are ready, remove from heat and add salt and pepper. Put the salt pork in 2 cups water, bring to a simmer and simmer 10 minutes; drain, rinse and dry. Cut the salt pork into small cubes and sauté with the garlic in the olive oil. Add the salt pork to the peas. Put about half of the peas through a food mill and let the purée fall into the pot. Add the macaroni and return the soup to the stove. When the pasta is tender, taste for seasoning. Serve the piping hot soup with grated Parmesan cheese.

SQUAB SOUP

(Zuppa di Piccione)

Serves 6

3 squabs
2 carrots, chopped
2 onions, chopped
1 small bunch celery, chopped
2 tablespoons oil
4 tablespoons butter
1 teaspoon salt
   pepper

2 medium tomatoes, peeled
2 cups dry white wine
12 slices homemade style bread,
   toasted
1 cup grated Parmesan cheese
1 tablespoon butter
   pinch nutmeg
1 quart clear broth

Wash the squabs carefully and blot dry with a dish towel. Lightly brown the squabs and chopped vegetables in a saucepan with the oil and 4 tablespoons butter, adding more if necessary. Season with the salt and pepper; add the peeled tomatoes and the white wine. When half the wine has evaporated, cover the saucepan and simmer over low heat for just over 1 hour. Take out the squabs, remove the meat from the bones and cut it into small slices. Place 4 slices of toast in the bottom of a well-greased oven-proof dish. Place half of the squab on the toast, together with one-third of the vegetable sauce, and one-third of the Parmesan cheese; dot with 1 teaspoon butter and sprinkle lightly with nutmeg. Cover this with another 4 slices of toast. Place the remaining squab and half of the remaining sauce and cheese on the bread; dot with 1 teaspoon butter and sprinkle with nutmeg. The last layer of bread can then be covered with all the remaining sauce, cheese and butter. Put the dish into a preheated 425° F. oven for 10 to 15 minutes, until brown and bubbling. Serve the squab casserole and the broth in separate dishes. Everyone at the table will serve himself with a portion of each, as desired.

TURKEY SOUP

(Zuppa di Tacchino)

Serves 6

⅔ cup (⅔ ounce) Italian dried mushrooms, soaked in warm water 30 minutes, squeezed dry
½ turkey (about 3¼ pounds) or 1 small roasting chicken
1 carrot, chopped
1 onion, chopped
½ bay leaf, chopped

   salt and pepper
4 tablespoons butter
1 pound chestnuts or 1 can (15½ ounces) peeled whole chestnuts
¼ cup flour
3 tablespoons dry marsala
   grated Parmesan cheese

Cut the mushrooms in strips. Clean and wash the turkey or chicken. Bone it, removing the skeleton at the opening of the thorax and the bones from the legs and wings. Cut the flesh into strips. Prepare a clear stock by boiling the turkey bones in 3 quarts of water with the chopped carrot, onion, bay leaf and salt and pepper to taste; strain. Melt 2 tablespoons of the butter in a saucepan; add the strips of turkey flesh and mushrooms. Stew slowly in a covered pan, adding the strained stock gradually. Husk the chestnuts and boil until tender, about 30 minutes; peel immediately and put them through a food mill. In another saucepan, melt the remaining 2 tablespoons of butter; stir in the flour. Cook until golden in color; remove from heat and add the boiling stock, reserving the turkey and mushrooms; stir until blended. Add the chestnut purée, reserved turkey and mushrooms and the marsala. Cook the soup for a further 10 minutes. Serve immediately with grated Parmesan cheese.

RICE AND BEAN SOUP

(Riso e Fagioli)   **Serves 6**

½ pound dried Lamon beans
1 onion
1 carrot
5 potatoes
¼ pound salt pork, finely cubed
6 tablespoons olive oil

½ tablespoon tomato paste
  salt and black pepper
1 onion, chopped
2 heaping tablespoons flour
1⅓ cups rice

This tasty soup is common to all regions of Italy. It is a national soup, although the method of cooking and the seasonings may vary. The most popular beans to use are those from Lamon in the Feltre region, as they are well known for their flavor and tenderness. Soak the beans overnight. The next day put them into an earthenware pot. Cover the beans with 3 quarts of cold water and add the onion, carrot and potatoes. Add the cubed salt pork to the beans along with 3 tablespoons of the olive oil and the tomato paste. Put the pot on the stove and let it boil for at least 3 hours, keeping the temperature steady. When it is cooked, add salt and black pepper to taste. Take all the vegetables and half of the beans from the soup and put them through a food mill, letting all the purée fall into the soup. In another saucepan sauté the chopped onion in the remaining 3 tablespoons oil until golden brown. Stir the flour into the onion and oil and let it cook. Strain this mixture into the bean soup, dipping the strainer into the soup so that none of the flavor is lost; throw out anything left in the strainer. When the whole beans are cooked and the soup has thickened, add the rice and cook until it is done but still firm.

BEEF SOUP

(Zuppa di Manzo)   **Serves 6**

2¼ pounds beef (preferably top
     round)
¼ cup olive oil
3 carrots, diced
3 potatoes, diced
2 onions, diced
1 celeriac, diced

1½ pounds green peas, shelled
½ cup dry red wine
  salt
2 tablespoons tomato purée
12 cups hot water
  pepper
  grated Parmesan cheese

Ask the butcher to cut the beef in 2¼-inch-thick slices, then cube it. Heat the olive oil in a casserole large enough to hold all the soup ingredients; lightly brown the cubed meat, carrots, potatoes, onions, celeriac, and the peas. Add the wine and cook over high heat to evaporate. When the wine is reduced, add salt to taste, the tomato purée, and the hot water. Bring to a boil, then reduce the heat and simmer gently for 2 hours, skimming the soup carefully from time to time. Add pepper to taste and correct the seasoning. Serve boiling hot, accompanied with grated Parmesan cheese.

RICE AND POTATO SOUP

DUMPLINGS IN BROTH

(Riso e Patate)   **Serves 6**

2½	quarts clear stock
2	tablespoons olive oil
	garlic
1	onion, chopped
½	pound cooked ham, diced

3	cups diced new potatoes
	salt
1⅓	cups rice
	chopped parsley
	grated Parmesan cheese

(Canederli in Brodo e Asciutti)   **Serves 6**

1¼	loaves stale bread
1⅓	cups milk
6	eggs
¾	cup melted butter
1	clove garlic, finely chopped
	finely chopped parsley

4	slices bacon, chopped
7	tablespoons bacon fat
	salt and pepper
1⅓	cups flour
	broth or butter and grated
	Parmesan cheese

Have some good clear stock ready on the stove. Put the oil in a saucepan; add the garlic, chopped onion and the fattest pieces of ham. Sauté gently, and when the onion is golden brown, add the diced potatoes and the rest of the diced ham. Stir to mix, add half of the hot stock, cover and let boil slowly. When the potatoes are cooked, put about one-third of them through a food mill, allowing them to fall back into the pot; then add the rest of the stock. Add salt to taste. When the soup boils add the rice and continue boiling it until it is soft. Before removing the soup from the heat add some chopped parsley. Serve very hot, accompanied with grated Parmesan cheese.

Crumble the bread and put it in a bowl. Bring the milk to the boil, pour it on to the bread and let stand until the milk is absorbed. Mix in the eggs one at a time, then the melted butter, garlic, parsley, bacon and bacon fat. Season with salt and pepper. Add enough flour to bind the mixture. Shape into large round balls and roll them in flour. These dumplings can be served in stock or as a separate course. Cook them in a large saucepan of boiling water. When they rise to the surface of the water, remove them with a slotted spoon. Two large dumplings and a ladleful of broth provide an excellent, nourishing soup, and two or three served seasoned with golden, melted butter and grated Parmesan cheese are an appetizing first course.

RICE AND FRESH PEA SOUP

RICE AND CHICKEN LIVER SOUP

(Riso con Piselli)   **Serves 6**

2½ quarts clear stock	3 strips bacon, chopped
½ onion, chopped	1⅓ cups rice
2 tablespoons olive oil	½ cup chopped parsley
3½ tablespoons butter	grated Parmesan cheese
3 pounds green peas, shelled	

(Riso in Brodo con Fegatini)   **Serves 6**

2 quarts clear chicken stock	4 tablespoons butter
1⅓ cups rice	salt
8 chicken livers	

Prepare a clear stock and keep it hot. Sauté the onion in the oil and butter until golden brown, then add the peas and chopped bacon; sauté lightly. Moisten with a ladleful of the stock. When all the liquid is absorbed, add the remaining stock. When the stock begins to boil, add the rice and cook for about 20 minutes or until the rice is fully cooked. Remove the soup from the heat and add the chopped parsley. Serve piping hot, accompanied with grated Parmesan cheese.

Put the chicken stock in an earthenware pot or large kettle and bring to the boil. Add the rice immediately and continue boiling uncovered, so that the grains of rice remain separate. Remove all green traces of gall from the chicken livers and wash well. Chop the livers into tiny pieces. Melt the butter in a skillet and cook the chopped livers over low heat for a short while or until just browned. As soon as the rice is cooked but still firm, add the chopped chicken livers to the soup with salt to taste. Serve at once piping hot.

SOUP WITH RICE DUMPLINGS

BEAN SOUP

(Polpettine di Riso)   **Serves 6**

2 cups rice	1 carrot, cut in julienne
½ pound Fontina cheese, diced	1 turnip, cut in julienne
3½ tablespoons butter	1 celeriac, cut in julienne
½ cup grated Parmesan cheese	3 or 4 lettuce leaves, cut in
3 egg yolks, beaten	julienne
3 heaping tablespoons flour	2 quarts clear stock
cooking oil	grated Parmesan cheese

Boil the rice until it is *al dente* (it should be done but still firm) in plenty of salted water. Place the diced Fontina cheese in a bowl. Drain the rice and scoop it over the cheese. The heat of the rice will melt the cheese. Mix well and add the butter, ½ cup grated Parmesan cheese and beaten egg yolks. Shape this rice mixture into small, round dumplings. Roll in flour before frying them in hot oil in a skillet. Remove the dumplings from the skillet when they are golden brown and drain on paper towels. Put the vegetables into a saucepan, pour in the stock and boil for 10 minutes. Add the dumplings and heat through. Ladle the steaming soup, with vegetables and dumplings, into warm soup plates. Serve accompanied with grated Parmesan cheese.

(Zuppa di Fagioli)   **Serves 6**

1⅓ cups dried white beans	¼ cup olive oil
4 potatoes, peeled	salt
2 carrots, chopped	freshly ground pepper
2 onions, chopped	dash olive oil
1 celeriac, chopped	12 slices home made style bread,
2 tablespoons tomato paste	toasted
½ pound rind or salt pork	

Soak the beans in water overnight. The following morning, put them in a large earthenware marmite, kettle or enameled cast iron casserole with the peeled whole potatoes, chopped vegetables, tomato paste, bacon rind or salt pork and olive oil. Bring to a boil, reduce the heat and simmer gently for about 3 hours. The salt should then be added. Remove the potatoes and two-thirds of the beans with a slotted spoon and put through a food mill back into the pot. Before removing the soup from the stove, test it for seasonings, grind in some pepper and add a dash olive oil. Serve the soup from the pot together with slices of toast.

LEEK SOUP

MUSHROOM SOUP

(Zuppa di Porri)   Serves 6

3¼ pounds leeks	6 potatoes, peeled
6 tablespoons butter	2½ quarts clear stock
3½ tablespoons olive oil	salt
¼ cup rice flour	grated Parmesan cheese

(Zuppa di Funghi)   Serves 6

2⅓ cups (2⅓ ounces) Italian dried mushrooms, soaked in warm water 30 minutes, squeezed dry	6 potatoes, peeled
3½ tablespoons olive oil	2½ quarts clear stock or water
5½ tablespoons butter	salt and freshly ground pepper
2 onions, chopped	½ cup light cream
2 heaping tablespoons rice flour	1 tablespoon butter
	chopped parsley
	grated Parmesan cheese

Cut the roots from the leeks, remove the green tops and leave only the tender white part of the leek. Wash well under running water to remove any traces of dirt. Pour boiling water over the leeks to remove the excess acid from them. Cut in half lengthwise, then into little strips about 2 inches long. Heat the butter and olive oil in a soup pot, add the leeks and sauté gently. Blend the rice flour in a little water, add it to the leeks together with the peeled whole potatoes and pour in the stock. Season with salt to taste and simmer for about 2 hours. At the end of the cooking time, remove the potatoes with a slotted spoon and pass them through a potato ricer or food mill back into the soup pot to thicken the soup. Keep the soup over low heat for about 5 minutes longer, then ladle it into soup dishes and serve accompanied with grated Parmesan cheese.

Cut the mushrooms into small pieces. Heat the oil and butter in a saucepan and sauté the chopped onions lightly; add the mushrooms. Blend the rice flour with a little cold water and add to the saucepan with the whole peeled potatoes. Let this cook a little to absorb the flavors, then add the stock. Season to taste with salt and pepper; simmer for at least 1 hour. Take the potatoes out and put them through a food mill back into the pot. Add the cream (which will thicken the soup), and stir in the butter (to make the soup shiny). Taste for seasoning and then let it simmer a few minutes longer. Garnish with chopped parsley and serve it piping hot, accompanied with grated Parmesan cheese.

TOMATO SOUP | SQUASH SOUP

(Zuppa di Pomodori)   Serves 6

- 1 onion, chopped
- 3 tablespoons olive oil
- 6 tablespoons butter
- 2½ tablespoons rice flour
- 6½ pounds ripe plum tomatoes, peeled, seeded and chopped
- 6 potatoes, peeled

- salt and pepper
- 2 quarts clear stock or water
- ½ cup light cream
- 1 tablespoon butter
- croutons
- grated Parmesan cheese
- cubed Fontina cheese

(Zuppa di Zucca)   Serves 6

- 1 onion, chopped
- 3½ tablespoons butter
- 3½ tablespoons olive oil
- 4½ pounds butternut squash, peeled, seeded and sliced
- 6 potatoes, peeled and sliced
- 2 tablespoons rice flour

- 3 quarts vegetable stock or water
- salt and pepper
- 1 cup light cream
- 1 tablespoon butter
- grated Parmesan cheese
- croutons

Sauté the chopped onion in oil and butter. Blend the rice flour smoothly with a little water. When the onion has become golden brown, add the tomatoes and the rice flour paste. Lastly add the whole potatoes. Add salt and pepper to taste and the stock, then cover the saucepan and let the ingredients simmer together for at least 1 hour. At the end of this time put enough of the potatoes through a food mill back into the pot to thicken the mixture. Let the soup simmer a little longer, slowly adding the cream. Stir in the butter. The butter will help to make the creamy soup smooth and shiny. Remove from the heat and serve in bowls, accompanied with croutons of bread sautéed in butter, grated Parmesan cheese and cubes of Fontina cheese.

Sauté the chopped onion in butter and oil, using a soup pot, until the onion is golden brown. Add the slices of squash and potatoes. Stir the ingredients with a wooden spoon and let the flavors of the vegetables blend while simmering. Mix the rice flour in a little cold water. Add it to the soup pot together with the vegetable stock. Season with salt and pepper to taste and simmer for about 1 hour, stirring from time to time. Put the soup through a food mill and return it to the stove to simmer. While it is simmering, add the cream and stir in the butter to give the creamy soup a smooth texture. Remove from the heat, pour into soup bowls and serve accompanied with grated Parmesan cheese and croutons of bread sautéed in butter or toasted in the oven.

VEGETABLE SOUP

PAVIA SOUP

(Zuppa di Verdura)   Serves 6

6 carrots	7 tablespoons olive oil
4 leeks	3 quarts water or clear stock
6 zucchini *or cabbage chopt*	1½ to 2 pounds short ribs
1 stalk celery	salt and pepper
3 pounds green peas, shelled	olive oil
1½ pounds lima beans, shelled	grated Parmesan cheese
6 potatoes	

(Zuppa alla Pavese)   Serves 6

7 cups clear meat stock	6 eggs
6 slices homemade style bread	white pepper
2 tablespoons butter	grated Parmesan cheese

This is a nourishing, digestible summer soup which can be served hot, cool or cold. Clean the vegetables thoroughly. Cut up all the vegetables, except the peas, beans and potatoes, in fine slices or cubes of uniform size. Peel and wash the potatoes, but leave them whole. Lightly sauté the vegetables (except the potatoes) in olive oil in a large saucepan. When the various flavors have blended, pour in the water or stock. Add the short ribs, season to taste, cover and simmer for about 2 hours. Put the potatoes through a food mill and add the purée of potatoes to the soup. Let it simmer a little more and taste for seasoning. Pour the soup into bowls and add a dash olive oil and a heaping tablespoon of grated Parmesan cheese to each bowl.

Prepare 7 cups of clear meat stock with no fat in it. Sauté the bread in the butter until golden brown on both sides, trying not to let the bread crumble. Put a slice of bread in each of six oven-proof soup plates. Break an egg on each slice of bread and put the plates into a preheated 450° F. oven to let the egg whites set quickly. When ready to serve, pour a ladleful of the hot stock into each plate. Add a pinch of freshly ground white pepper to each plate. Serve the soup accompanied with grated Parmesan cheese.

ASPARAGUS SOUP

(Zuppa di Asparagi)   Serves 6

6 potatoes	9½ cups clear stock or water
4½ pounds asparagus	salt
1 onion, chopped	3 egg yolks
3 tablespoons olive oil	grated Parmesan cheese
3 tablespoons butter	½ cup light cream
¼ cup rice flour	

Peel and wash the potatoes. Scrape, peel and thoroughly wash the asparagus. Cut the tips off the asparagus and reserve. Cut up the tender part of the asparagus stalks. Sauté the chopped onion in oil and butter in a soup pot until golden brown. Add the chopped asparagus stalks and cook gently to bring out the flavor. Blend the rice flour in a little cold water, add to the soup pot with the potatoes, then pour in the stock or water. Add salt to taste. Simmer slowly for at least 1 hour and then put the soup through a food mill. Return the soup to the stove, add the asparagus tips and cook for a further 15 minutes. Beat the egg yolks in a soup tureen with a little grated Parmesan cheese and the cream. Slowly pour the soup into the tureen and mix well to thicken it. Serve it hot in elegant soup bowls, accompanied with additional grated Parmesan cheese.

LENTIL SOUP

(Zuppa di Lenticchie)   Serves 6

1 cup lentils	pinch thyme
⅝ pound chestnuts	pinch marjoram
¼ cup olive oil	olive oil
6 slices bacon, chopped	freshly ground pepper
½ tablespoon tomato purée	10 slices homemade style bread,
½ cup dry white wine	sautéed in oil
salt and pepper	

This is a lentil soup prepared in the Abruzzi. Soak the lentils in cold water for 24 hours. The following day pick out any lentils which have risen to the surface of the water. (Quick-cooking lentils do not need soaking.) Boil the lentils in a saucepan for 1½ to 2 hours. Meanwhile, cut a gash on the flat side of each chestnut. Place with a little oil in a preheated 350° F. oven until they can be easily husked and peeled. Cut them into small pieces. Sauté the chestnuts in oil in a saucepan together with the chopped bacon. Dilute the tomato purée with the white wine. When the bacon is golden, add the diluted tomato purée, salt, pepper and the herbs tied in a cheesecloth bag which can later be removed. Cook this sauce slowly. Add the cooked lentils to the sauce with as much of the water in which they have been cooked as is necessary for the quantity of soup required. Let the soup cook slowly for a further 15 minutes. Remove the bag of herbs. Serve the soup piping hot in earthenware soup dishes, seasoned with a dash olive oil, freshly ground pepper and accompanied with slices of homemade style bread sautéed in oil.

PASTA AND VEGETABLE SOUP	PASTA AND EGG SOUP

(Pastina con Verdura)   Serves 6

2 tablespoons butter	2 quarts clear meat stock
3 potatoes, peeled and cubed	2 cups small pasta shapes
3 zucchini, unpeeled and cubed	salt and pepper
1 pound (generous) tomatoes, peeled	grated Parmesan cheese

(Pastina Legata all'Uovo)   Serves 6

2 quarts clear meat stock	4 eggs
2 cups small pasta shapes	1 cup grated Parmesan cheese

Melt the butter in a saucepan over low heat. Add the potatoes, zucchini and tomatoes and let the flavors of the ingredients blend. Pour in ½ cup of the meat stock. Let this cook for a short while, then add the rest of the stock. As soon as the soup comes to the boil add the pasta, which cooks in 5 minutes. Taste the soup for seasonings. Pour the piping hot soup into dishes and serve accompanied with grated Parmesan cheese.

Bring the stock to the boil, add the pasta and cook for 5 minutes. Beat the eggs and Parmesan cheese in a soup tureen. Pour the hot soup very slowly into the soup tureen, stirring all the time. Serve hot.

BEEF-PAPRIKA SOUP

CLEAR FISH SOUP

(Zuppa di Manzo con Paprica)   Serves 6

- ½ pound onions, sliced
- 1 clove garlic, chopped
- 4 slices bacon, chopped
- 1¾ pounds beef chuck or round, cubed
- salt
- 1 teaspoon paprika
- 3 green peppers, sliced
- 4 potatoes, cubed
- 3 plum tomatoes, seeded and peeled
- 2½ quarts boiling water
- 3 Italian pork sausages, thinly sliced
- 12 slices stale dark bread

(Zuppa di Pesce Marechiaro)   Serves 6

- 5½ pounds fish (sole, bass, halibut, mussels, clams, etc.)
- 1 cup olive oil
- 2 onions, chopped
- 1 carrot, chopped
- 1 stalk celery, chopped
- 2 cloves garlic (inner buds removed)
- salt and pepper
- ½ cup red wine
- 1 pound canned tomatoes
- 6 slices bread

Sauté the onion and garlic with the bacon in a cauldron, if possible, or heavy pot. Add the beef to the cauldron. Brown the beef, then season it with salt and the paprika. Stir well and cover so that the meat can absorb the flavorings of the spicy sauce. Cook slowly for 15 minutes. Add the peppers, potatoes and tomatoes to the meat and sauce. Cover with the boiling water and simmer for 2½ to 3 hours. At the end of the cooking time, add the slices of Italian pork sausage. Simmer for about 10 minutes longer. Taste for seasoning and test the meat to see if it is tender. Suspend the cauldron from a tripod and serve the soup with slices of stale dark bread.

Scale, gut, bone and wash the fish very carefully. Slice the sole. Brush and scrape the mussels and clams and sauté in a saucepan with half of the oil until the shells open. Strain the remaining liquid and reserve it. Prepare some fish stock by boiling the large fish heads, bones and any trimmings, together with one of the chopped onions, the carrot and celery. Keep the stock warm. Brown the garlic and the remaining onion in the remaining oil over a high flame. Add the fish to the dish, starting with the firmest bits, season with salt and pepper and add the wine. When the wine has evaporated, add the reserved liquid from the clams and mussels. Add the tomatoes and the fish stock. Bring to a boil, reduce the heat and simmer for 15 minutes. Toast the bread in the oven. Rub a little garlic over each slice and put one in each soup plate. Arrange the pieces of fish and seafood on the bread and pour in the broth.

CREAM OF FISH SOUP

MUSSEL SOUP

(Crema di Pesce)   Serves 6

5½ pounds firm sea fish
 1 pound mussels
 ¾ cup olive oil
 2 onions, chopped
 4 potatoes, chopped
 2 carrots, chopped
   pinch saffron
 1 cup dry white wine

 4 ripe tomatoes, seeded and
     chopped
2½ quarts water or fish stock
 ½ bay leaf, chopped
     chopped parsley
12 slices bread, toasted and
     rubbed with garlic

(Zuppa di Cozze)   Serves 6

60 mussels
 1 cup dry white wine
 2 pounds sea squab
 1 carrot, chopped
 1 onion, chopped
 1 stalk celery, chopped
   salt

   cayenne pepper
 ¼ cup olive oil
 ¼ cup flour
 5 anchovy fillets, chopped
     chopped parsley
12 slices bread sautéed in oil

Clean and wash the fish very carefully. Cut into pieces. Wash, scrub and "beard" the mussels. Put them in a saucepan with ¼ cup of the oil over high heat to open. Remove the shells and reserve the flesh. Put the chopped onions, potatoes and carrots in a large saucepan with ¼ cup of the oil. Cook, stirring, over high heat, then reduce the heat and simmer. Blend the saffron with a little white wine and add to the vegetables. Stir well, cover the saucepan and continue simmering. Sauté the pieces of fish in the remaining oil. Add the fish to the vegetables, together with the tomatoes and simmer; when mixture becomes dry, add the remaining white wine and the water or fish stock. Cook for about 1 hour, then strain the soup in a colander. Sieve the pieces of fish into the soup, removing any bones, and add the chopped bay leaf. Put this purée on the stove, stir it well, add the mussels and let it heat through. Serve the soup with chopped parsley and toasted bread rubbed with garlic.

Wash, scrub and "beard" the mussels. Drain well and put them into hot wine to steam for 5 minutes or until they open. Clean and wash the sea squab and cut the flesh into pieces. Cover the sea squab with 2½ quarts water, add the chopped vegetables and boil, adding salt and cayenne pepper to taste. Continue boiling for 30 minutes, then put the sea squab and vegetables through a grinder; sieve to purée. Strain the fish stock. Heat the oil in a saucepan, add the flour and cook until golden. Add the chopped anchovy fillets, then gradually add some of the strained fish stock. Mix well so that the sauce thickens without becoming lumpy. When it is thickened and smooth, pour it into the strained stock, together with the sieved fish purée. Add the mussels and cook the soup for a few minutes longer to let the flavors mingle. Serve it in soup plates, sprinkled with chopped parsley and accompanied with sautéed bread.

ROAST LEG OF LAMB, BAKER'S STYLE   STUFFED FILLET OF BEEF

(Agnello alla Fornaia)   Serves 6

1 leg of lamb (3½ pounds)	5 tablespoons butter
salt and pepper	white wine
1 teaspoon rosemary	2½ pounds new potatoes
6 tablespoons olive oil	polenta, cut into cubes*

(Filetto di Bue Farcito)   Serves 10

1 fillet of beef	· 1 onion, chopped
1 dowel (1½ inches in diameter), the	salt and pepper
same length as the meat, end sharp-	¼ teaspoon sage
ened to a point	½ teaspoon rosemary
1 pound chicken livers	½ cup dry marsala
5 tablespoons olive oil	1¼ cups melted butter

This traditional roast is the only one cooked in the oven. At one time, when housewives did not have ovens, the baker was asked to prepare and cook the roast. Cut the leg of lamb open and season the inside of the meat with salt and pepper and the rosemary to taste. Tie the meat into its original shape. Put it in a roasting pan and sprinkle with the olive oil. Dot with the butter. Roast in a preheated 450° F. oven, sprinkling occasionally with the white wine. Cook the new potatoes in the pan with the roast to absorb the flavors. The roast will be cooked in 1½ hours. Remove the string and cut good-sized slices of the meat. Arrange the slices on an oval dish; sprinkle with a little of the pan gravy. Serve garnished with the potatoes, cubed polenta and curly endive leaves.

* Prepare the polenta following the recipe on page 11 but cube instead of slicing and warm without the cheese in a preheated 250° F. oven.

Remove all traces of fat from the fillet and cut away any stringy bits at the sides. Fold the thin end under and tie the fillet at intervals, making a compact roll. Work the dowel carefully through center of the fillet, leaving it in place. Put the fillet in a large roasting pan and roast it in a preheated 450° F. oven for 15 to 25 minutes, depending upon the degree of rareness you like. Remove from the oven, cool, remove the strings and roll it in aluminum foil. Refrigerate for a few hours. Clean the chicken livers carefully, removing all greenish bits of the gall. Wash the livers and dry them on paper towels. Heat the olive oil and sauté the onions in a saucepan. Add the chicken livers and season with salt and pepper and the sage and rosemary. Add the marsala and cook for about 3 to 4 minutes. Put the liver mixture through a grinder at least twice. Beat the mixture with a wooden spoon and continue beating while adding the melted butter. Let the pâté solidify a little. Remove the dowel from the center of the fillet, and, using a pastry bag fitted with a large round tip, pipe the chicken liver pâté into the hole made by the dowel. When the pâté has become firm, cut the meat into slices. The contrast between the pink meat and the white stuffing makes an attractive dish.

Meat

In this section there is no distinction made between the types of meat, and so recipes for chicken appear side by side with those for pork, the ones for turkey next to veal, and so on. The choice of meats and the cuts recommended need not be followed exactly. What is important is the preparation of the meat, the method of cooking it and the time required. This information is necessary where certain diets may be practiced or the time available may be limited. Modern production and marketing techniques mean that the methods of preparation and cooking are often the only means of providing any individuality in dishes. At one time the term "chicken" had a precise meaning and was distinct from spring chicken, capon, cockerel, pullet and hen, but today these distinctions no longer exist. Accordingly where the recipes give a precise term, or state a specific item, they may be freely interpreted.

ROAST VENISON

(Capriolo al Forno) **Serves 6**

1 leg of venison (3½ pounds)
7 tablespoons bacon fat
½ teaspoon sage
½ teaspoon rosemary
8 juniper berries, crushed

salt and pepper
6 tablespoons olive oil
polenta, cut in small squares and
    sautéed in butter*

(This dish calls for roebuck and red chicory, both of which are unavailable in the United States. Venison and curly endive, however, are satisfactory substitutes.)

Cut open a leg of venison, wash and dry it. Skin the leg, trying to keep the skin intact. Rub the leg with the bacon fat, sage, rosemary, crushed juniper berries and salt and pepper. Cover the herbs with the skin and tie the leg into its original shape. Put the oil in a skillet over high heat and brown the meat on all sides. When the meat is browned, roast it in a preheated 350° F. oven for 1 hour, basting occasionally with its own juices. Just before removing the meat from the oven, untie the string and remove the skin. Let the meat brown a little longer and cut into slices. Place the slices of meat on an oval serving dish and garnish with curly endive leaves and small squares of sautéed polenta. Pan roast potatoes and buttered green peas go well with this dish.

* Prepare the polenta following the recipe on page 11, up to the point of slicing it. Cut it into small squares and sauté in butter.

ROAST VEAL WITH VEGETABLES

(Arrosto di Vitello con Verdure) **Serves 6**

1 onion, chopped
1 celeriac, chopped
1 carrot, chopped
1 clove garlic, chopped
6 tablespoons olive oil
2 tablespoons flour
5½ tablespoons butter

1 loin of veal (4½ pounds), boned,
    rolled and tied
¼ teaspoon sage
½ teaspoon rosemary
1 cup white wine
    grated Parmesan cheese

Sauté the chopped vegetables in a pan or oven-proof dish in the oil. Knead the flour and butter together and add to the vegetables to thicken the sauce. Season the veal with salt and pepper and the sage and rosemary. Brown it with the vegetables on all sides and put the dish in a preheated 325° F. oven for 2 hours. Pour the wine over the meat and turn frequently, basting it with the pan juices as it roasts. When the veal is ready, remove it from the pan and cut the strings. Put the sauce through a food mill to purée the vegetables. Slice the veal and put it on a warm serving dish. Pour the puréed sauce over the slices. Sprinkle with grated Parmesan cheese. Pan roast potatoes and broiled tomatoes are excellent accompaniments with this dish.

ROAST BEEF

(Roast-Beef) **Serves 6 to 8**

½ onion, chopped
 1 carrot, finely sliced
 6 tablespoons butter
¼ pound beef suet, chopped
 1 sirloin roast (3½ pounds)

½ pound sliced bacon, parboiled
      10 minutes
¼ cup flour
     salt and pepper

Sauté the onion and carrot in an ovenproof dish with 2 table-spoons of the butter and the suet. Smear the roast with the remaining butter. Lay the bacon slices lengthwise along the roast and tie in position with string. Dredge the roast in flour and brown in the oven-proof dish with the onion and carrot. Season with salt and pepper and transfer the dish to a pre-heated 325° F. oven. Baste frequently with the pan juices and roast 1¾ hours. To be properly cooked, the beef should be golden on the outside and pinkish inside. Slice the cooked roast and serve on a hot platter. Braised spinach and boiled potatotes are excellent accompaniments.

ROAST PORK TENDERLOIN

(Lombo di Maiale al Forno) **Serves 6**

 3 pounds pork tenderloins
 1 teaspoon rosemary
¼ teaspoon sage
 2 cloves, garlic, crushed
     salt and pepper

12 slices bacon
 6 tablespoons olive oil
 4 tablespoons butter
½ cup white wine
     chicken stock

Choose lean pork and parboil it for 15 minutes. Mix the rose-mary, sage and garlic with salt and pepper. Push the herbs and seasonings into the meat with the tip of a teaspoon. Tie the bacon slices around the meat. Heat the oil and butter over high heat and brown the roast on all sides. Pour the wine over the meat and put it into a preheated 325° F. oven for 30 min-utes. Turn the meat frequently to brown it evenly, basting with the pan juices. When the pork is cooked, remove the bacon. Slice the meat and arrange it on a warm platter garnished with lettuce leaves. Dilute the pan juices with a little chicken stock and pour into a gravy boat to serve with the roast.

ROAST LOIN OF PORK

ROAST GUINEA HEN

(Carré di Maiale al Forno)   Serves 6

1 loin of pork (6 pounds)
3 carrots, cut into strips
  salt
2 cloves garlic
6 tablespoons olive oil

6 tablespoons butter
  freshly ground pepper
½ cup white wine
½ cup milk

(Faraona al Forno)   Serves 4

1 guinea hen (about 3¼ pounds)
¼ teaspoon sage
1 teaspoon rosemary
  salt and pepper
1 clove garlic

10 slices bacon
6 tablespoons olive oil
4 tablespoons butter
½ cup dry white wine

Pierce the meat in several places with a sharp knife and insert the strips of carrot and some salt. Rub the pork with a clove of garlic, then tie it in several places to help it keep its shape. Sauté the pork in an oven-proof dish over high heat with the oil and butter, browning it evenly. Season with salt and freshly ground pepper and add the wine. When the wine has evaporated, pour the milk over the roast and put it into a preheated 325° F. oven. Watch carefully during cooking, turning the meat regularly and basting it with the pan juices. When cooked, slice the pork into chops. Arrange the chops on a warm platter and pour the sauce over them. Garnish with leaves of Bibb lettuce.

Rub the inside of the hen with the sage, rosemary and salt and pepper. Rub garlic over the hen to add flavor, cover it with bacon slices and truss with string. Heat the oil and butter in a deep saucepan over high heat and brown the bird. Add the white wine. When the wine has evaporated, put the pan into a preheated 375° F. oven. Roast the bird for 1½ hours, turning it frequently and basting it with the pan juices. When the bird is tender, remove it from the oven and cut in quarters. Reassemble it on a warm serving dish to appear whole. Salad and pan roasted new potatoes are excellent accompaniments.

(Petto di Tacchino al Forno)   Serves 6

1 turkey breast (3 pounds)
1 teaspoon rosemary
¼ teaspoon sage
6 tablespoons olive oil
1 onion, finely chopped
1 carrot, finely chopped

½ celeriac, finely chopped
4 tablespoons melted butter
salt and pepper
½ cup dry white wine
chicken stock

(Faraona in Salsa Peverada)   Serves 4

1 guinea hen (2½ to 3 pounds)
salt and pepper
¼ teaspoon sage
1 clove garlic

6 tablespoons butter
6 tablespoons olive oil
½ cup dry white wine

For the Piquant Sauce

¼ pound chicken livers
2 slices soft salami
3 anchovy fillets
1 clove garlic (inner bud removed)
¼ pound pickled green peppers
¼ cup olive oil

salt and pepper
2 tablespoons chopped parsley
clear stock
juice of 1 lemon
wine vinegar

Tie the turkey breast into a round shape with string. Rub with the rosemary and sage. Heat the oil in an oven-proof dish and sauté the chopped vegetables lightly. Add the turkey breast; sprinkle it with the melted butter and season with salt and pepper. Sauté it gently in the oil with the seasonings. Add the wine and when it has evaporated put the dish into a preheated 325° F. oven for 2 hours. Turn the breast frequently to brown on all sides and baste with the pan juices. Remove the string a short time before taking the meat from the oven. Serve garnished with Bibb lettuce hearts. Dilute the pan-gravy with a little hot chicken stock if necessary and pour into a gravy boat to serve with the breast. Pan roasted potatoes may be served with this dish.

Rub the inside of the bird with salt and pepper, the sage and the garlic. Smear the breast with the butter. Place the hen in a pan with the oil and put it into a preheated 375° F. oven for 1½ hours. During the cooking, sprinkle with the white wine, then baste frequently with the pan juices. **To prepare the sauce:** Remove all traces of gall from the chicken livers. Chop the chicken livers, salami, anchovies, garlic and pickled peppers. Put them in a saucepan and sauté lightly in the olive oil, adding salt, pepper and the chopped parsley. Add a little clear stock to the sauce as needed during cooking. Pour the hot sauce into a sauce boat, then add the lemon juice and a dash wine vinegar. When the hen is tender, remove it from the oven and quarter it. Reassemble it on a warm serving dish so that it appears whole. Serve it accompanied with the piquant sauce.

ROAST MOCK SUCKLING PIG

ROAST PHEASANT, RICH MAN'S STYLE

(Tacchinella in Porchetta)　　　　　　　Serves 6

1 small turkey (about 4 pounds), boned	10 slices bacon
2 cloves garlic	6 tablespoons olive oil
salt and pepper	6 tablespoons butter
1 teaspoon rosemary	½ cup dry white wine

(Fagiano Arrosto alla Ricca)　　　　　　Serves 4

salt and pepper	4 tablespoons melted butter
1 pheasant (about 3¼ pounds)	6 tablespoons olive oil
2 tablespoons chopped sage leaves or 1 teaspoon ground sage	¼ cup grappa
	30 pitted black olives
10 juniper berries	½ cup hot stock
6 slices bacon, blanched in boiling water 10 minutes	

To bone the bird, put it on a wooden board and cut down the back. Remove the wing tips. Using a small sharp knife, scrape the meat from the carcass. Remove the leg and wing bones and cut the leg tendons, being careful not to break the skin. Flatten the carcass on the board, first with the palm of the hand, then with a meat pounder. Rub the garlic over the meat and season the inside with salt and pepper and the rosemary. Roll up the turkey and skewer it. Tie the bacon slices over the turkey and season it once more. Put the roll into a pan and brown it over high heat in the oil and butter. Add the white wine and let it evaporate. Put it into a preheated 400° F. oven immediately to continue cooking. Turn it often and baste it well with its own juices to keep the surface of the meat moist. Cook for 1½ hours or until the juices run clear when turkey is pricked with a fork. Slice the roll and arrange on a warm platter garnished with lettuce leaves, ripe tomatoes, fennel and carrots.

Rub salt and pepper inside the bird and place the sage leaves and juniper berries inside. Cover the breast of the bird with the bacon and tie in place with string. Skewer the bird to help keep its shape. Sprinkle the butter and oil over the bird and brown in a pan over high heat. As it is browning, season with salt and pepper, pour in the grappa and add the black olives. When browned, put the pheasant with its seasonings into a preheated 350° F. oven. Turn the bird during cooking, basting it frequently with the pan juices to keep moist. Cook for 1 hour. Remove the pheasant to a warm platter and add the hot stock to the roasting pan. Stir well with a wooden spoon. Put the gravy into a sauce boat and add an additional tablespoon of butter and a few drops of lemon juice. Arrange the pheasant attractively on a serving dish. Garnish the platter with black olives and lemon slices and serve the pheasant accompanied with the sauce.

(Faraona alla Creta)   Serves 6 to 8

½ teaspoon sage
1 teaspoon rosemary
2 cloves garlic
  salt and pepper
2 guinea hens (about 2 pounds each)

¼ cup olive oil
6 slices bacon
2 double sheets greased aluminum
  foil
10 pounds clay*

(Pollo Cotto nel Pane)   Serves 6

2 cups lukewarm water
14 cups flour
¾ teaspoon rosemary
6 sage leaves
3 cloves garlic
3 halves chicken (about 1¼
  pounds each)
  salt and pepper

3 slices bacon, blanched in boiling
  water 10 minutes
3 carrots, cut in julienne
1 onion, cut in julienne
½ celeriac, cut in julienne
½ cup chopped peeled tomatoes
1 egg, beaten

Put sage, rosemary, garlic, salt and pepper inside each bird. Season the outside of the birds with salt and pour 2 tablespoons olive oil over each. Place 3 bacon slices on each bird. Tie a string around the birds at the wings and at the legs. Wrap each bird in well-greased double sheets of aluminum foil. Place the birds on a baking sheet and pack the clay around them about ½ inch thick. Put the clay-covered birds in a preheated 250° F. oven and cook for about 3 hours. When the birds are ready, the clay will be white, dry and hardened. Bring the guinea hens to the table on a broad chopping board. Break the clay open with a hammer and serve the birds to your guests.

* Moist ceramic clay is available in bags in art supply stores.

Blend the water and flour to a smooth dough. Keep aside a small amount for decoration. Divide the remainder of the dough into three pieces and roll out until it is ½ to ¾ inch thick. Place ¼ teaspoon rosemary, 2 sage leaves and a clove of garlic on each piece about one-third of the way in (you will want to be able to fold the dough over the chicken so the seal is on the side). Put the chicken halves on top of the herbs, season with salt and pepper and place a bacon slice on top of each chicken. Top each one with one-third of the vegetable strips and tomatoes. Fold the dough over the chicken, dampen the edges and seal the ends and side. Brush the top of the dough with the beaten egg. Make a decoration for the top of each loaf and fasten them down with toothpicks. Make two steam holes on the top of each loaf with a skewer. Put the pastry-encased birds on a floured baking sheet in a preheated 425° F. oven. Cook them for about 1 hour or until the juice begins to bubble through the steam holes. Serve them at the table unopened. Cut an oval piece from the top and serve the chicken in front of your guests.

(Pernici alla Boscaiola)   Serves 6

6 partridge	sage
salt and pepper	rosemary
24 juniper berries	1 bay leaf
12 slices bacon	30 black olives
6 tablespoons olive oil	½ cup dry white wine
4 tablespoons melted butter	6 pieces polenta, sautéed*

(Bocconcini di Vitello alla Cacciatora)   Serves 6

½ to ¾ pound mushrooms, sliced, or	2¼ pounds boned veal shoulder
1¼ cups (1¼ ounces) Italian	or breast, cut in small pieces
dried mushrooms, soaked in warm	salt and pepper
water 30 minutes, squeezed dry	2 cups dry white wine
6 tablespoons olive oil	½ pound tomatoes, peeled and
4 tablespoons butter	chopped
1 onion, finely chopped	1 cup clear stock
2 carrots, finely chopped	mashed potatoes (page 145)
1 celeriac, finely chopped	

Season the inside of the birds with salt, pepper and juniper berries. Cover the birds with the bacon and truss. Heat the oil in a pan and place the birds in it, taking care to keep them separate. Pour some melted butter over the breast of each bird. Tie together a tiny bunch of sage and rosemary with the bay leaf and add with the black olives to the pan. (The herbs can be removed at a later stage.) Brown the birds quickly, pour the wine over them and place them in a preheated 450° F. oven to roast for 30 minutes. Before taking them from the oven, remove the strings and bacon and let them brown a little longer. Sauté six pieces of polenta. Put these on a serving dish, place a partridge on each piece and pour the sauce over the birds and polenta. Serve garnished with slices of lemon and the black olives used in the cooking of the partridge.

* Prepare the polenta following the recipe on page 11 up to the point where it is sliced. Cut six pieces, each large enough to hold one partridge, and sauté in butter. Sautéed bread may be substituted instead.

Put the mushrooms in a saucepan with the oil and butter. Put over medium heat and when hot, add the onion, carrots, celeriac and the pieces of veal. Sauté lightly until golden brown and season with salt and pepper. Add the wine and when it has partially evaporated, add the chopped tomatoes and the clear stock. Cover the saucepan, reduce the heat and cook for just over 1 hour. When the veal is tender, remove from the heat. Check the sauce for thickness, adding more stock or reducing further, and seasoning, then pour the mixture into a warm oval dish. Garnish with piped mounds of mashed potatoes.

ROUND STEAK WITH PIZZAIOLA SAUCE   STEWED RABBIT, HUNTER'S STYLE

(Costata alla Pizzaiola)   Serves 6

¼ cup olive oil
2 cloves garlic (inner buds removed)
1 onion, chopped
1 round steak (2½ to 3 pounds)
¼ cup flour
   salt and pepper

1 teaspoon oregano
1 pound tomatoes, peeled, seeded
   and excess moisture squeezed
   out
   clear stock

(Coniglio alla Cacciatora)   Serves 3 to 4

1 rabbit (about 2¾ pounds)
¼ cup olive oil
7 tablespoons butter
1 onion, chopped
¼ cup flour
2 cups white wine
1 pound tomatoes, peeled, seeded
   and excess moisture
   squeezed out

¾ to 1 pound mushrooms, finely
   sliced
   salt and pepper
   boiled potatoes
   polenta*

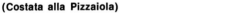

Heat the oil in a large skillet and sauté the garlic and onion briefly. Dredge the beef with flour and brown it with the garlic and onion, seasoning it with salt and pepper. Mix the oregano with the tomatoes and add them to the beef. As soon as they come to a boil, reduce the heat and cover the saucepan. Simmer the meat for about 30 minutes in the sauce, turning it occasionally. If the sauce becomes too thick, add a little clear stock. When the steak is tender, slice it and arrange on a warm platter. Cover with the sauce and serve.

Wash the rabbit and dry it well. Cut it into serving-size pieces. Heat the oil and butter in a saucepan. Sauté the chopped onion briefly, then add the pieces of rabbit and brown lightly. Sprinkle with the flour, stirring well to incorporate it. Add the white wine. As soon as the wine has evaporated, add the tomatoes and then the mushrooms. When the mixture comes to a boil, season with salt and pepper, cover and reduce the heat. Simmer slowly for about 1 hour or until the rabbit is tender. If the sauce becomes too thick, add some clear stock. Boil some potatoes, then cook them for a few minutes in the rabbit sauce. Serve the rabbit and potatoes accompanied with hot polenta.

* Prepare polenta following the recipe on page 11, but cook, stirring, for 30 minutes only. This is not served in slices but as cornmeal mush.

STEWED CHICKEN, HUNTER'S STYLE | CHICKEN IN ASPIC

(Pollo alla Cacciatora)   Serves 6

1 chicken (about 3¼ pounds)
½ cup olive oil
1 onion, chopped
1 carrot, chopped
1 stalk celery, chopped
2 tablespoons butter
¼ cup flour
½ to ¾ pound mushrooms, finely
    chopped or 1⅓ cups (1⅓
    ounces) Italian dried mush-
    rooms, soaked in warm
    water 30 minutes, squeezed
    dry

salt and pepper
2 cups dry white wine
½ pound tomatoes, peeled and
    sliced

(Pollo in Gelatina)   Serves 4 or 5

1 chicken (about 3½ pounds)
2 veal knuckles
½ teaspoon salt
1 quart water
1 onion, chopped

1 carrot, chopped
1 stalk celery, chopped
2 cups cooked peas, chilled
    Bibb lettuce leaves
    butter

Wash the chicken and cut in serving pieces. Heat the oil in a large skillet and sauté the chopped onion, carrot and celery lightly. Add the pieces of chicken. Keep the heat high and turn the chicken gently with a wooden spoon until it is browned all over. Cream the butter and flour with a fork until it is smooth. Add this to the chicken together with the mushrooms, salt and pepper. Add in the wine and when this has evaporated add the sliced tomatoes. When the mixture comes to a boil, cover and reduce the heat. Simmer for at least 1 hour, stirring occasionally. When the chicken is tender, correct the seasoning. Serve the chicken from a heated dish. Corn meal mush (polenta) accompanied with a sauce of red and green peppers is often served with this dish.

Divide the chicken into eight even-sized pieces. (To do this, leave the wings attached and cut the breast, minus the ribs, in half crosswise. The ribs and back may be discarded after cooking.) Clean the veal knuckles, singe and wash well. Put the chicken in a pot with the salted water, chopped vegetables and veal knuckles. Bring to a boil, then reduce the heat and simmer uncovered for 1 hour, skimming carefully so as to obtain a clear stock. Remove the chicken and vegetables, but leave the knuckles to cook, covered, for an hour longer. This will make the stock concentrated and gelatinous. Let the pieces of chicken cool and when the stock is done, taste for seasoning. Strain it through a damp cheesecloth. Arrange the chicken neatly in an oval mold, cover with the jellylike stock and refrigerate until set. When ready to serve, dip the mold into hot water for 2 or 3 seconds and invert onto a serving dish. Surround the aspic with green peas. Garnish the edge of the dish with Bibb lettuce leaves and piped creamed butter.

OXTAIL STEW

(Coda alla Vaccinara)   Serves 6

1 oxtail (about 4½ pounds)
½ pound bacon, chopped
¼ cup olive oil
1 carrot, chopped
1 onion, chopped
1 stalk celery, chopped
  salt and pepper
2 cloves garlic, crushed

  pinch nutmeg
1 cup dry white wine
1 pound tomatoes, peeled, seeded
    and excess moisture
    squeezed out
¼ cup pine nuts
1 tablespoon white raisins

Cut the oxtail at the joints of the vertebrae. Put the pieces in a bowl and leave under gently flowing cold water for at least 3 hours. Put the pieces of oxtail into a saucepan, cover with cold water and bring to a boil. Reduce heat and simmer for 2 hours. Remove the pieces of oxtail and drain. Heat the chopped bacon in a saucepan with the oil and brown the chopped carrot, onion and celery. Add the pieces of oxtail. Season with salt and pepper and add the crushed garlic and nutmeg. Pour in the white wine and when it has partially evaporated, add the tomatoes. Cover, reduce the heat and simmer gently for about 1 hour. Before removing from the stove, check the tenderness of the oxtail and the seasoning and thickness of the sauce, adding more stock or reducing the sauce further. At the last minute add the pine nuts and white raisins. Pour this Roman delicacy onto a warm serving dish and serve piping hot.

ROUND STEAK WITH TOMATOES

(Manzo al Pomodoro)   Serves 6

1 pound onions, finely sliced
¼ cup olive oil
½ pound bacon, minced
1 rump steak (about 2¾ pounds)
¼ cup flour
  salt and pepper

1 clove garlic
2 cups red wine
2¼ pounds tomatoes, peeled,
    seeded and drained
  polenta*

Sauté the sliced onions in a large skillet with the oil and minced bacon. Before the onions change color, add the steak and brown on both sides. Turn it, flour it, and season it with salt, pepper and two drops of crushed garlic from a garlic press. Pour the wine over the meat and let it evaporate slightly. Add the tomatoes mixed with the basil and reduce the heat. Simmer slowly for 1½ to 2 hours. If the sauce becomes too thick, dilute it with a little clear stock. Test the meat with a fork to see if it is tender. When tender, slice and arrange on a warm serving dish. Cover with the sauce. Garnish the edges of the serving dish with slices of hot polenta.

* Make the polenta as in the recipe on page 11 up to the point of slicing it. Cut in the desired shapes, sprinkle with melted butter and warm in a preheated 250° F. oven.

(Manzo Farcito)   Serves 6

1 rolled beef rump (3¼ pounds)	1 onion, chopped
1 carrot	¼ cup olive oil
3 Italian sausages	salt and pepper
¼ cup flour	4 cups red wine

(Osso Buco con Funghi)   Serves 4 to 6

1 onion, finely chopped	¾ cup white wine
1 carrot, finely chopped	3 tablespoons tomato purée
1 celeriac, finely chopped	clear stock
½ cup olive oil	1 tablespoon chopped rosemary
6 veal shanks (about ½ pound each)	2 tablespoons chopped parsley
3 tablespoons flour	1 clove garlic
salt and pepper	mushroom sauce*

Ask the butcher to prepare a rolled rump with a regularly-spaced cavity running the length of it. Insert a peeled, washed carrot and the sausages. Sprinkle the beef with flour. Using a casserole, brown the chopped onion in oil over low heat, then add the beef. Turn often to brown evenly. Season it with salt and pepper, then pour in the wine (preferably Barolo). Cover the casserole, reduce the heat and simmer slowly for about 3 hours. Taste for seasoning during the cooking and check that the sauce is thickening properly. The stuffed beef is ready when fork tender. Cut it into slices and arrange the slices attractively on a heated, rectangular dish. Sprinkle the gravy over the meat and serve immediately. This dish is excellent accompanied with cornmeal mush.

Brown the onion, carrot and celeriac in the oil in a casserole. Dredge the shanks in flour and add them to the vegetables. Brown evenly and then set upright to retain the marrow. Season with salt and pepper and pour the wine over them. When the wine has partially evaporated, dilute the tomato purée with a little clear stock and pour it over the meat. When the liquid begins to boil, cover the casserole, reduce the heat and simmer slowly for 1½ to 2 hours. Before removing from the heat add the chopped rosemary and parsley, then two drops of garlic from a garlic press. Place the meat in a warm oven-proof dish and cover with the mushroom sauce.

* Use the sauce for Tagliatelle with Mushroom Sauce on page 36.

VEAL WITH TUNA FISH SAUCE

VEAL, CREOLE STYLE

(Vitello Tonnato)   Serves 6

2½ pounds boneless rolled rump of veal ½ onion
  1 teaspoon salt   1 stalk celery
  ½ carrot   ½ bay leaf

For the sauce
2 cans (6 ounces each) tuna fish in oil, 3 eggs, hard cooked
  flaked   olive oil
  juice of 2 lemons   salt
3 ounces anchovy fillets   capers in vinegar

(Fesa alla Creola)   Serves 6

  1 pound onions, finely sliced salt and pepper
  ½ cup olive oil 1 cup white vinegar
  7 tablespoons butter 1 cup heavy cream
2¾ pound boneless rolled leg of veal

Put the veal in a pot with boiling water to cover. Add the salt, carrot, onion, celery and ½ bay leaf. Reduce the heat and simmer for about 1½ hours or until the veal is tender. Let it cool in its own stock. When cool, wrap the veal in aluminum foil and refrigerate until ready to serve.

To prepare the sauce: Soak the flaked tuna fish in a bowl containing the lemon juice for 1 hour. Put the tuna through a fine sieve or into an electric blender together with the anchovy fillets and the hard cooked eggs. If using a blender, purée at low speed. Mix a little oil into the purée and season with salt to taste. Take the veal from the refrigerator and cut it into thin slices. Arrange them in layers on a chilled platter. Cover the slices with the tuna fish sauce, reserving a little to pipe in festoons around the edge of the platter. Serve accompanied with a small bowl of capers pickled in vinegar.

Sauté the onions in the oil and butter in a casserole. Before the onions change color add the veal. Sauté it with the onions, turning it so that it browns evenly. Season with salt and pepper and pour in the vinegar. As soon as the vinegar has evaporated, cover the saucepan and reduce the heat. Cook gently for 1½ to 2 hours. During cooking turn the meat and check on the thickness of the sauce. When the onions are almost dissolved, remove from the pan and put them through a food mill. Put the onion purée into a bowl with the cream and stir gently. Add this mixture to the veal to cook over high heat for 1 minute. Remove the veal and slice it. Serve in a warm oven-proof dish covered with the sauce.

ROAST VEAL LOIN

PARTRIDGE, CHARCOAL BURNER STYLE

(Lombo di Vitello al Forno) Serves 6

3¼ pounds boneless rolled veal loin	rosemary sprig
salt and pepper	1 sage leaf
garlic	1 cup dry white wine
6 tablespoons olive oil	mashed potatoes (page 145)
5 tablespoons butter	

(Starne alla Carbonara) Serves 6

3 partridge	5 sage leaves
salt and pepper	24 green Spanish olives, pitted
12 juniper berries, crushed	½ cup dry white wine
12 slices bacon	Bibb lettuce leaves
¼ pound salt pork, chopped	lemon wedges
6 tablespoons butter	carrot slices

Season the veal with salt and pepper. Rub some garlic over the meat and put into a pan with the oil, butter, a sprig of rosemary and the sage leaf. (Remove herbs after cooking.) Cook the meat over high heat, turning until it is browned evenly. Transfer the pan to a preheated 325° F. oven for about 1½ hours. Baste the roast frequently, at first with the white wine and when that is used, with the pan juices. When the veal is tender, take it from the oven. Slice it and arrange the meat on a warm platter. Garnish with piped mashed potatoes and serve immediately. Braised spinach and broiled tomatoes go very well with this roast.

(Bibb lettuce may be used as a garnish in place of the red chicory shown in the photograph.)

Season the inside of the birds with salt, pepper and the crushed juniper berries. Roll up each bird in slices of bacon and tie the legs close to the body. Put the chopped salt pork and 2 tablespoons of the butter into a deep saucepan. Arrange the partridge in the pot. Melt the remaining butter and sprinkle it over the breasts. Sauté the birds, turning to brown evenly. Add the sage leaves and the olives. Pour the white wine over the birds and when it has evaporated, cover the saucepan and simmer over low heat for 45 minutes. Arrange the birds on a serving dish and garnish with the green olives, Bibb lettuce leaves and wedges of lemon topped with carrot slices.

(Trippa e Fagioli)   **Serves 6**

3 pounds honeycomb tripe*
1 onion, sliced
1 stalk celery, sliced
1 carrot, sliced
½ cup olive oil
  salt and pepper

½ cup peeled, seeded and chopped
  tomatoes
2 cups dry white wine
2 tablespoons brandy
  boiled white Spanish beans

(Manzo Stracotto)   **Serves 6**

2¾ pounds top round of beef
1 clove garlic
  salt and pepper
2 carrots, chopped
2 onions, chopped
1 celeriac, chopped

¼ cup olive oil
1 bay leaf
¼ cup flour
1 quart strong red wine
  polenta slices, toasted*

Clean the tripe thoroughly under running water, drain and then cut into fine strips. Cook the tripe in 6 quarts of boiling salted water for 2 hours. Sauté the onion, celery and carrot in a large saucepan with the oil. Stir the vegetables, keeping them moist, and when they are golden brown add the tripe. Brown the tripe, season it with salt and pepper and add the tomatoes. Stir in the wine. As soon as the mixture starts to boil, cover the saucepan and cook slowly for 2 hours over low heat. A little clear stock can be added to the sauce if it becomes too thick. When the tripe is cooked, taste for seasoning and stir in the brandy. Arrange the tripe on a warm serving dish surrounded by tender boiled beans.

* As bought in many butcher shops, tripe has been preboiled. If that is the case, omit the boiling and simply cut it into fine strips.

Rub the beef with garlic, season it with salt and pepper and tie it in shape with string. Sauté the carrots, onions and celeriac in a deep saucepan with the oil. Put the meat in; add the bay leaf and more salt. Brown the meat evenly over medium heat, sprinkling it with the flour. When it is well browned, pour the wine over it. As soon as the wine comes to a boil, cover the saucepan, reduce the heat to very low and cook for 3 to 4 hours. When the meat is tender, remove it from the saucepan and keep it hot. Put the vegetable gravy through a food mill, then return it to the heat to thicken. Remove the string from the meat and slice it. Arrange the slices on a warm serving dish and pour the thick gravy over them. Serve accompanied with slices of freshly-toasted polenta.

* Prepare polenta according to the recipe on page 11 up to the point of slicing it. Cut into the desired shapes and toast, sprinkled with melted butter, in an oven-proof pan under the broiler.

PIGS' FEET WITH BEANS | BEEF IN RED WINE

(Zampini di Maiale con Fagioli)   **Serves 6**

1 pound white Spanish beans	¼ cup olive oil
6 pigs' feet	2 slices bacon, chopped
salt	pepper
bouquet garni	½ teaspoon sage
1 onion, chopped	¼ cup flour
1 clove garlic, minced	2 cups red wine

(Manzo al Vino Rosso)   **Serves 6**

2¾ pounds top round of beef	½ pound bacon, minced
salt and pepper	1 pound tomatoes, peeled
1 bay leaf	¼ cup flour
pinch nutmeg	polenta*
3½ cups strong red wine	Bibb lettuce
5 onions, finely sliced	

Soak the beans in water overnight. Scrape the pigs' feet, singe and wash them, first in cold water, then in boiling water. When they are completely clean cut them in half lengthwise and boil them in a saucepan of salted water with a bouquet garni. Cook for 2 hours until tender. Remove the bones and chop the meat in small pieces. Sauté the onion and garlic in the oil and chopped bacon over medium heat. Add the soaked beans, seasoned with salt, pepper and the sage. Sprinkle the flour over the beans and pour in the wine. When the liquid comes to a boil, cover the saucepan and cook over low heat for 1½ hours. Taste to see if the beans are sufficiently tender and seasoned. When almost done, add the meat from the pigs' feet. Cook the beans and chopped meat for 30 minutes longer. Serve piping hot in an oven-proof dish.

(Bibb lettuce may be used in place of the red chicory in the photograph to garnish the polenta.)

Place the beef in a large bowl and season with the salt, pepper, bay leaf, nutmeg and red wine. Marinate for 12 hours, turning occasionally if necessary. Drain the meat and strain the marinade. Sauté the onions in a casserole with the bacon. When the onions are golden brown, add the meat and brown it evenly over medium heat. Add the tomatoes; sprinkle the flour over the meat while turning it. Gradually increase the heat so any moisture will evaporate. When the meat is browned, pour the strained wine over it. When the liquid comes to a boil, cover the saucepan, reduce the heat and cook the meat slowly until the gravy becomes concentrated. Invert the hot polenta in the center of a warm serving dish and surround it with slices of the beef. Degrease the gravy and pour it over the meat. Serve immediately.

* Make the polenta according to the recipe on page 11 but put it into a round bowl and turn it out while still hot.

HARE IN RED WINE

BOILED CALF'S HEAD

(Lepre al Vino Rosso)   **Serves 4**

1 hare (about 3¼ pounds)
1 pound onions, sliced
½ cup olive oil
¼ pound bacon, chopped
  salt
1 green chili pepper, chopped
6 tablespoons flour
4 cups strong red wine
  clear stock
  polenta*

(Testina di Vitello Bollita)   **Serves 6**

1 calf's head (about 2¾ pounds)
½ cup vinegar
½ bay leaf
1 onion, studded with 1 clove
1 tablespoon salt
¼ cup olive oil
  green sauce (page 215)
  boiled onions

Cut the hare into pieces, keeping the fleshiest parts, and wash it. Sauté the onions in the oil and chopped bacon. Add the pieces of hare and brown them with the onions. Stir the salt and chili pepper into the hare and onion mixture. Sprinkle the pieces of hare with flour, covering them all well. Pour the red wine over the hare, cover the saucepan and reduce the heat to low. Cook slowly for 2 hours. Watch it carefully while cooking and if the sauce becomes too dry, add some clear stock. Before removing the hare from the heat, pass the onions through a food mill. Put the purée back into the saucepan with the hare and let it simmer for a few minutes, seasoning with salt if necessary. Arrange the hare over the hot polenta on a warm platter, cover with the onion sauce and serve immediately.

* Prepare the polenta according to the recipe on page 11 but cook for 30 minutes only. Turn the polenta onto the platter immediately.

Bone the calf's head and roll the meat up in the skin. Bind it with kitchen twine, wrap it in a linen cloth and put it into a saucepan. Cover with water and add the vinegar, ½ bay leaf, onion and the salt. Bring the water to a boil, pour in the olive oil and boil for at least 3 hours. When the meat is tender, remove the head from the stock. Unwrap the linen cloth and slice the meat. Arrange the slices on a warm serving dish. Serve accompanied with green sauce and tiny boiled onions.

(Cima alla Genovese)   Serves 6 to 8

1 veal stomach (3¼ pounds)	marjoram
½ pound veal	8 eggs
10 ounces calf's brains	grated Parmesan cheese
2 tablespoons butter	2 ounces shelled pistachio nuts
¼ cup olive oil	boiling clear stock
1 clove garlic, chopped	2 pounds veal casing
salt and pepper	

(Lingua e Pollo Bolliti)   Serves 6

salt	1 calf's tongue (about 1½ pounds)
1 chicken (about 2¾ pounds)	rosemary sprig or small pinch
½ onion	dried rosemary
1 carrot	horseradish sauce (page 219) or
1 stalk celery	pepper sauce (page 222)
	mashed potatoes (page 145)

Ask the butcher for a clean stomach from a calf. Wash the veal and brains and cut them into pieces. Heat the butter, oil and garlic in a small saucepan and sauté the veal and brains, seasoning them with the salt, pepper and marjoram. Brown the meat lightly. Put it through a grinder into a large bowl. Beat the eggs well with a little salt and enough grated Parmesan cheese to make a thick consistency. Add this and the whole pistachio nuts to the ground meat. Stir gently, and when all the ingredients are well mixed, fill the calf's stomach with the mixture. Leave some space at the opening to allow the stuffing to expand during the cooking. Wrap the stomach in a linen cloth, tie it and place it in a pot of boiling clear stock. Reduce the heat and simmer for nearly 3 hours. Cool the stuffed veal in the stock. When the veal has cooled, remove it from the linen cloth and wrap it tightly with the veal casing. Reroll the stuffed veal in the linen cloth and refrigerate for several hours before cutting it into thin slices. If desired, the stuffed veal can be eaten hot as soon as it has been cooked in the stock.

Salt the inside of the chicken, truss it and put into a pot of boiling salted water with onion, carrot and celery. The water should just cover the bird. Cook at a slow boil, carefully removing the scum to keep the stock clear. Adjust the cooking time according to the size and quality of the bird. Cook the calf's tongue at the same time in another pot. Cover it with cold salted water and add rosemary sprig. Cook for about 2 hours. When the chicken and the tongue are tender, remove them from the heat. Cut them up in any way you like, arrange on a warm serving dish and serve accompanied with mashed potatoes and horseradish sauce or hot pepper sauce.

BOILED BEEF

BOILED TURKEY

(Manzo Bollito)   **Serves 6**

3 pounds beef rump	salt
1 carrot	green sauce (page 215)
1 celeriac	basil sauce (page 217)
1 onion	horseradish sauce (page 219)
10 cups boiling water	

(Tacchina Bollita)   **Serves 6 to 8**

1 turkey (about 5 pounds)	1 carrot
salt	1 celeriac
½ pound ham, sliced	summer stew of peppers
1 onion	(page 234)

Add the beef and vegetables to the boiling water. Bring the water back to a boil, reduce the heat and cook at a slow boil for 2 hours or more, carefully skimming the stock of scum to keep it clear. Towards the end of the cooking time, season with salt. When the beef is tender, remove it from the stock and slice. Arrange the slices on a warm serving dish and sprinkle with some salt and 1¼ to 1½ cup of the hot stock. Serve accompanied with green sauce, basil sauce and horseradish sauce.

Ask the butcher to bone the turkey for you. Spread it out on a chopping board and flatten it with the palm of your hand, then use a meat pounder lightly to flatten it further (take care not to damage the skin). Sprinkle salt over the inside of the bird and place the ham inside. Roll up the turkey and sew the edge closed with a needle and white thread. Bind the full length of the turkey with kitchen twine. Add enough water to a pot to just cover the rolled turkey. Salt it lightly and add the vegetables. Heat, and when the water comes to a boil, add the rolled turkey to the pot. Cook for about 2 hours over a slow, regular heat, skimming the stock continuously to keep it clear. At the end of the cooking time, test for tenderness with a fork. When the rolled turkey is tender, remove it from the pot and slice. Serve it on a warm platter accompanied with a dish of stewed peppers.

PIG'S FOOT, SAUSAGE, POTATOES

SAUSAGE AND MASHED POTATOES

(Zampone e Cotechino)   Serves 8 to 10

   1 pig's foot (about 2 pounds)
   2 Modena or cotechino sausages
      (about 1¼ pounds each)

For the mashed potatoes
1½ pounds potatoes, unpeeled   4 tablespoons melted butter
     salt   ½ cup hot milk

(Cotechino e Puré)   Serves 6 to 8

   2 Modena or cotechino sausages   mashed potatoes (page 145)
      (about 1½ pounds each)

Pierce the pig's foot and the sausages with a small skewer. Put them into a bowl of cold water and let them stand overnight. The next day, cut the pig's foot in half and cook in boiling water for at least 3 hours. Wrap each of the sausages in muslin and sew firmly closed with thick thread. Lay the sausages on the bottom of a large saucepan. Cover them with cold water and simmer for at least 3 hours. When cooked, remove the muslin. Slice while still hot.

To prepare the mashed potatoes: Boil the potatoes in an uncovered saucepan with a little salted water until tender. Peel them while still hot and put through a food mill and into a saucepan containing the melted butter. Beat the mixture well with a wooden spoon. Beat in enough of the hot milk to give the desired consistency. When the purée is smooth and well mixed, mound it in a warm serving dish and serve with the pig's foot and sliced Italian sausages. Lentils are excellent with this dish.

Soak the sausages overnight in cold water. Remove them from the water, loosen the string at the top and pierce the skin with a skewer at several points. Wrap each sausage in muslin and tie them closed. Put them in a large saucepan with enough cold water to cover them. As soon as the water begins to boil, turn the heat down as low as possible. Simmer for 3 hours, skimming the water occasionally. Remove the sausages when cooked; slice them. Reassemble them on a layer of mashed potatoes on a warm platter. Pipe a design around the edge of the platter with some of the potato. Decorate with slices of carrot and zucchini.

LARGE SALAMI IN SAUCE

CHICKEN COOKED IN BEER

(Salama da Sugo)   **Serves 6**

2 salame da sugo (about 1¼   mashed potatoes (page 145)
   pounds each)

(Pollo alla Birra)   **Serves 6**

1 chicken (about 3¼ pounds)   salt and pepper
2 large onions, sliced   2 cups beer
¼ cup olive oil   1 cup heavy cream
6 tablespoons butter   mashed potatoes (page 145)
¼ cup flour

(Salama da sugo is very difficult to obtain in the United States.)

Wash the salami in lukewarm water, removing any trace of mold and any marks brought about by the mellowing process. Soak them in cold water for a few hours. Put them in a small canvas bag, tie the top of the bag and hang it from a long wooden spoon laid across the rim of a tall, wide pot. Put enough water into the pot to cover the salami and cook them thoroughly. Cover the pot and bring the water slowly to a boil; cook for 4 hours. (The skins should not burst if these instructions are followed carefully). At the end of the cooking time, remove the salami from the canvas bag and cut the string at the top of each salami. Spoon the meat inside them into nests of hot mashed potatoes on a warm serving dish.

Clean and wash the chicken. Sauté the onions lightly in the oil and butter in a large saucepan. Sprinkle the chicken with flour and place it in the saucepan. Sauté it, turning to brown evenly, for about 10 minutes. Put the chicken in a casserole, season with salt and pepper and pour the beer over it. Cover and cook in a preheated 350° F. oven for 1¼ hours. If necessary, moisten with a few spoonfuls of water during cooking. When the chicken is cooked, purée the onions in an electric blender or put through a food mill. Return the purée to the casserole and heat, mixing with the cream. Add salt to taste. Serve the chicken and sauce on a warm dish accompanied with mashed potatoes or boiled rice.

VEAL CUTLETS IN TOMATO SAUCE

VEAL CUTLETS WITH HAM

(Scaloppine di Vitello al Pomodoro)   **Serves 6**

1 onion, chopped	6 sage leaves, finely chopped
¼ cup olive oil	6 veal cutlets
2¼ pounds tomatoes, peeled, seeded	½ cup flour
and drained	5 tablespoons butter
salt and pepper	¼ cup dry white wine

(Scaloppine al Prosciutto)   **Serves 6**

6 veal cutlets (about 6 ounces each)	6 slices ham, chopped
salt and pepper	¼ teaspoon dried sage
¼ cup flour	½ cup dry white wine
6 tablespoons olive oil	½ cup hot stock
6 tablespoons butter	

Sauté the onion lightly in a saucepan with the oil. Add the tomatoes to the onions and let them absorb the onion flavor. Cook slowly, adding salt, pepper and the sage leaves. Flatten the veal cutlets with a meat pounder, season them with salt and pepper and coat them lightly with flour. Melt the butter in a large skillet and brown the cutlets on both sides over a high heat, keeping them well apart. Sprinkle the white wine over them and when it has evaporated add the tomato sauce. Taste for seasoning. Cook the sauce and cutlets together for a few minutes, keeping the lid on the pan to bring out the full flavor. Arrange the cutlets in sauce on a hot oven-proof dish and serve at once.

Lightly beat the veal cutlets with a meat pounder and remove any stringy parts. Season them with salt and pepper, dip them in flour and sauté them on both sides in a large skillet with the oil and butter. Add the ham and sage to the skillet with the white wine. Cover the skillet, reduce the heat and simmer the cutlets gently in the sauce for about 20 minutes. As soon as the chops are ready arrange them on a warm serving dish. Put the pieces of ham on top of the veal. Increase the heat to high and dissolve the gravy in the bottom of the skillet with the hot stock. Pour this hot gravy over the cutlets and serve at once.

(Cervella al Burro)   Serves 6

1¾	pounds calf's brains
	lemon slices
	salt
1	bay leaf
1	onion, chopped
1	carrot, chopped

¼	cup vinegar
	pepper
¼	cup flour
6	tablespoons butter
	lemon juice

(Costoletta alla Milanese)   Serves 6

6	veal loin chops
	salt and pepper
2	eggs, beaten
1	cup dry bread crumbs

¼	cup grated Parmesan cheese
½	cup flour
7	tablespoons butter

Rub the brains with lemon and soak them in cold water for 30 minutes. Drain and remove any membranes or little red veins. Rub the brains once more with lemon and soak them in cold water again until they become very white. Boil the brains in slightly salted water with the bay leaf, onion, carrot and vinegar. Drain and cut the brains into pieces. Season them with salt and pepper. Dip each piece in flour and sauté them in 4 tablespoons of the butter until golden brown on all sides. Remove from the heat, arrange them on an oven-proof dish and keep hot. When ready to serve, sprinkle the brains with the remaining melted butter and drops of lemon juice.

The chops should be cut from the veal loin, each one attached to a bone. Flatten them with a meat pounder, season with salt and pepper and dip the meat in the beaten eggs. Mix the bread crumbs with the Parmesan cheese and flour. Coat each chop with this mixture, pressing it in well with the palm of the hand. Melt the butter in a large skillet and when it is golden and spluttering, sauté the chops until they are golden brown. Reduce the heat and cook the chops for about 20 minutes, turning to brown evenly. When they are tender, arrange them on an oval serving dish with a paper frill around the top of each chop. This dish is excellent served with fried potatoes and lemon wedges.

FRIED CHICKEN BREASTS

(Petti di Pollo Fritti) **Serves 6**

6 chicken breasts, halved and boned
   with wing bone remaining
  lemon juice
6 slices prosciutto
6 slices fontina cheese
½ cup flour

3 eggs, beaten
1 cup dry bread crumbs
  cooking oil
  salt
  mashed potatoes (see page 145)

Wash the chicken breasts in water and lemon juice and dry them with paper towels. Place them on a chopping board and beat lightly to flatten them as much as possible. Cut away any cartilage. Wrap a slice of prosciutto and a slice of fontina cheese around each chicken breast and fix them in place with a toothpick. Dip the chicken breasts first in flour, then in egg and finally in bread crumbs. Leave the wing bones free of egg, flour and bread crumbs. Fry the rolled chicken breasts in hot oil until golden brown, drain on absorbent paper and sprinkle with a little salt. Arrange the breasts on a bed of mashed potatoes and decorate the wing bones with paper frills.

BREAST OF CHICKEN FANTASY

(Petto di Pollo Fantasia) **Serves 6**

3 chicken breasts with wings, boned
  and halved
  juice of 1 lemon
  salt and pepper
½ cup flour
10 tablespoons butter
¼ pound mushrooms or ½ cup dried
  Italian mushrooms, soaked in warm
  water 30 minutes, squeezed dry

2 cloves garlic (inner buds
  removed)
2 tablespoons chopped parsley
7 tablespoons grated Parmesan
  cheese
2 eggs, beaten

Remove the wing tips and wash the chicken breasts in water and lemon juice; dry them with paper towels. Beat them with a meat pounder, leaving the little wing bone bare. Season the chicken breasts with salt and pepper, then dredge lightly with flour. Melt 5 tablespoons of the butter in a large skillet and when it is golden, brown the chicken breasts lightly on both sides. Reduce the heat and simmer for about 20 minutes. Remove the breasts from the skillet and place on a chopping board. Cut a neat hole, about 1⅛ inches in diameter, from the center of each breast. Grind the meat taken from the hole with the mushrooms, garlic and parsley and mix with the Parmesan cheese and salt and pepper. Bind the mixture with the beaten eggs. Make six round croquettes with this mixture and put them in the empty space in each chicken breast. Melt the remaining butter in the skillet and sauté the stuffed chicken breasts until they are a little browner. Arrange the breasts on a heated oval serving dish and pour the juices in which they were cooked over them. Decorate the wing bones with paper frills.

BROILED CHICKEN BREASTS

CALF'S LIVER, VENETIAN STYLE

(Petti di Pollo alla Griglia)   Serves 6

3 whole chicken breasts, boned and
    halved
   juice of 1 lemon

salt and pepper
3 tablespoons olive oil

(Fegato di Vitello alla Veneziana)   Serves 6

½ cup olive oil
1 pound medium-size white onions,
    finely chopped

1¾ pounds calf's liver, sliced
     salt and pepper
6 slices polenta, toasted*

Wash the chicken breasts in water and lemon juice; dry them
with paper towels. Flatten each breast lightly with a meat
pounder and remove the stringy part at the center. Put them
on a red-hot broiling rack and reduce the heat immediately.
Turn them as soon as the roasted flesh is easily removed from
the rack. Season them with salt and pepper and brown on the
second side. Sprinkle with olive oil and arrange them on a
warm serving dish. Potato chips, buttered peas and stuffed
tomatoes au gratin are excellent accompaniments for this
dish.

Heat the olive oil in a saucepan over medium heat. Add the
onions and when they are golden brown, add the liver. Increase
the heat and cook the liver quickly to prevent it from becoming tough. Stir gently during cooking and season with salt and
pepper. As soon as it is cooked, serve the liver immediately
on a warm serving dish surrounded by slices of freshly
toasted polenta:

* Make the polenta according to the recipe on page 11 up to the point of
slicing. Cut in the shapes desired and toast it under the broiler.

(Bistecca alla Fiorentina)   Serves 6

3 porterhouse steaks   pepper
      (about 1¾ pounds each)   salt
   olive oil   lemon wedges

(Il Piatto del Boscaiolo)   Serves 6

 6 Italian sausages   rosemary
 6 small pork cutlets   ¼ cup olive oil
12 mushrooms   slices of polenta, toasted*
      salt and pepper

The secret of a perfectly cooked Florentine steak lies in the speed of the cooking. The meat must be well browned on the outside but bloody inside. Soak the steaks in olive oil and pepper. Drain them and lay them on a blazing hot broiling rack. Reduce the heat immediately. Turn steaks halfway through cooking time; when drops appear on the surface of the meat, sprinkle salt on both sides. Garnish the steaks with wedges of lemon and serve with grilled mushrooms.

Cut the sausages in half and pound the pork cutlets until thin. Wipe the mushrooms gently with a damp linen cloth and separate the stems from the caps. Trim the stems. Wrap the cutlets around the mushroom stems, then put them on skewers with the mushroom tops and sausages, alternating the ingredients. Place the skewers on a very hot broiling rack. Reduce the heat immediately and cook the ingredients slowly. Turn the skewers so that the ingredients are evenly cooked. Season with a little salt and pepper. Serve very hot, sprinkled with a little rosemary-flavored oil. Place slices of toasted polenta on the serving dish beside the skewers.

* Make the polenta according to the recipe on page 11 up to the point of slicing it. Cut into the desired shapes, sprinkle with butter and toast under the broiler.

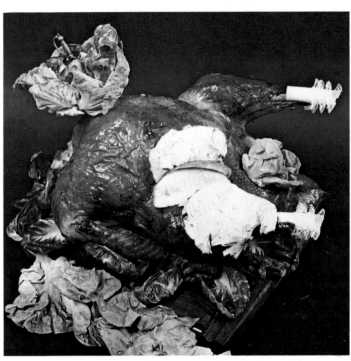

(Piatto San Lorenzo)   Serves 6

½ cup olive oil
3 tablespoons hot mustard
1 clove garlic (inner bud removed),
   crushed
1 rosemary sprig or small pinch dried
   rosemary
1 sage sprig or small pinch dried sage

1 teaspoon vinegar
   salt and pepper
6 pork chops (about 3 ounces each)
6 pieces fillet of beef
   (about 2 ounces each)
6 thick slices bacon
6 mushroom caps

(Tacchina allo Spiedo)   Serves 6

1 turkey (about 5 pounds)
   sage
   rosemary
3 cloves garlic

   salt and pepper
12 slices bacon
½ cup olive oil

Prepare the sauce an hour before broiling the meat. Mix the oil, mustard, crushed garlic, rosemary, sage, vinegar, salt and pepper in an earthenware dish. Let the sauce stand until it is time to serve it. Pound the pork chops with a meat pounder, flatten the fillets with the palm of the hand, spread out the slices of bacon and wipe the mushroom caps carefully. Put all these ingredients on a very hot broiling rack, remembering that the ingredients which need the longest cooking time should be put on first. Reduce the heat as soon as the meats become brown, turning them frequently to brown them evenly. Sprinkle salt and pepper over them. As soon as the meats are ready, arrange them on a serving dish. Remove the crushed garlic and the sage and rosemary sprigs from the sauce. Serve the grilled meats and mushrooms accompanied with the highly seasoned sauce.

Season the inside of the bird with sage, rosemary, garlic, salt and pepper. Truss the bird and spread the bacon over the breast. Tie bacon in place with white thread. Put the turkey on a spit and cook for 1½ to 2 hours. Put the oil and some salt and pepper in a little dish and while the turkey is turning, brush it with the oil. When the turkey is cooked and golden brown, remove the thread and the bacon from the breast. Carve the bird neatly. Arrange on a warm serving dish and decorate with lettuce leaves. Cover the tips of the drumsticks with paper frills.

VEAL CUTLETS WITH GORGONZOLA CHEESE   LONGOBARD GRILL

(Nodini di Vitello al Gorgonzola)   **Serves 6**

6 veal cutlets	5 tablespoons butter
5 tablespoons olive oil	¼ pound Gorgonzola cheese
salt and pepper	green sauce (page 215)

Soak the veal cutlets in the oil. Drain them and put them on a very hot broiling rack until brown on both sides. As they are turned, shake some salt and pepper over them. Cream the butter and cheese together with a fork. Shape this mixture into rounds. Place a round on each cutlet as it is taken from the broiler. Arrange the cutlets on a warm serving dish and serve immediately, accompanied with green sauce.

(Piatto del Longobardo alla Griglia)   **Serves 6**

6 slices fillet of beef (about 2 ounces each)	1 red pepper, sliced
6 slices pork loin (about 2 ounces each)	salt and pepper
6 slices calf's liver (about 2 ounces each)	½ cup olive oil
3 Italian sausages	creamy horseradish sauce (page 219)
sage leaves	mustard
polenta squares*	lemon wedges

Gently flatten the slices of fillet, loin and calf's liver. Cut the sausages in half. Put a selection of meats on the skewers, alternated with sage leaves, squares of polenta and slices of red pepper. Put them on a red-hot broiling rack. Reduce the heat immediately. Turn the skewers to cook the ingredients evenly. Sprinkle them with salt and pepper and brush with oil. Serve the broiled meats on a gaily colored plate accompanied with creamy horseradish sauce and mustard. Garnish with lemon wedges.

* Prepare the polenta according to the recipe on page 11. When ready to slice, follow the directions above.

BEEF ROLLS, CALABRIAN STYLE

SPIT-COOKED MIXED GRILL

(Rollatini alla Calabrese)   Serves 6

6 slices fillet of beef	6 slices bacon
6 slices ham	6 slices spicy salami
6 slices mozzarella cheese	salt

(Spiedini di Carni Miste)   Serves 6

1½ pounds hog casing	6 pieces boned loin of lamb
6 quails	chopped sage
6 pieces pork liver	chopped rosemary
1 Italian pork sausage, chopped	salt and pepper

Flatten the slices of fillet first with the palm of the hand, then lightly with a meat pounder. Lay a slice of cooked ham and a slice of mozzarella cheese over each fillet. Roll these up and place two to a skewer, alternating the beef rolls with rolled bacon slices and rolled salami. Put the skewers on a very hot broiling rack. Reduce the heat immediately. Turn the skewers to ensure even cooking; season the meat with salt. The meat will be cooked and golden brown in a short time. Serve the beef rolls very hot.

Soak the hog casing in water for 1 hour, then cut into squares. Choose firm quails with white flesh and truss them. Put them on a chopping board with the pieces of liver, sausage and lamb and sprinkle all the ingredients with sage, rosemary, salt and pepper. Wrap each piece of meat with its flavorings in one of the squares of hog casing. Put these little parcels of meat on a skewer with the quails and cook for about 30 minutes. When they are cooked and golden brown, remove them from the skewer. Arrange them on a serving dish and serve piping hot with French fried potatoes.

Fish

Italians are not great fish eaters, in comparison with people in the United States. However, despite this apparent lack of interest they achieve delicious results in preparing and cooking fish. In the maritime regions of Italy, fish dishes, when served, are perhaps the greatest attraction on the menu. The methods used are usually simple and rarely elaborate. They bring out the different flavors of fresh-water as compared with salt-water fish, with the latter shown to particular advantage. Naturally there are some Italian fresh-water fish which are not found in American rivers and others which are not easily obtainable. However, there is usually a more common alternative which can be used instead; for example trout is similar to powan. There are other salt-water fish which have rather euphemistic common names, such as dog fish which is usually known as rock salmon, and these are indicated in the recipes.

In this section there are some recipes which not only make use of fresh-water fish but are indeed created solely for that particular kind of fish. Much of the success of these dishes can be attributed to the combination of fish with dry white wine, and many Italian wines are used in this way to bring out the delicate flavor of the fish. They may also be served chilled with the meal, in which case they demonstrate one of the most successful unions of food and drink.

STUFFED CODFISH, VICENZA STYLE   # STUFFED SQUID

(Baccala' alla Vicentina)   Serves 6

1¾ pounds dried cod, soaked 24 hours in 6 changes of water	2 onions, sliced
3½ ounces salted anchovies	1 cup olive oil
lemon slices	7 tablespoons butter
handful parsley	pepper
4 cloves garlic (inner buds removed)	1 quart milk
¾ to 1 cup grated Parmesan cheese	½ cup heavy cream
flour	6 slices polenta, toasted*

(Seppie Ripiene)   Serves 6

6 medium-sized squid	salt and pepper
3 cloves garlic	¼ cup olive oil
¼ cup chopped parsley	½ cup dry white wine
¼ cup bread crumbs	6 slices polenta, toasted*

Skin the softened cod; cut in on one side, open it as you would a book and bone. Scrape the salt from the anchovies, wash them with slices of lemon and bone. Chop the anchovies with a handful of parsley and 1 clove of the garlic, then mix in the grated Parmesan cheese. Pack the inside of the cod with this mixture. Close up the piece of cod again, pressing the edges together to seal well. Cut into broad slices and dip them in flour; arrange the slices closely together in a well-greased oven-proof dish. Sauté the sliced onions and the remaining garlic (chopped) lightly in the oil and butter. When they are beginning to change color, pour them over the cod. Add pepper to taste, then cover the fish and onions with milk and cream. Cover and cook, either in a preheated 350° F. oven or over low heat for 2 to 3 hours, until the milk has been absorbed. Sprinkle with additional chopped parsley and a dash olive oil. Serve piping hot, accompanied with slices of toasted polenta.

* Make the polenta according to the recipe on page 11. Cut in the desired shapes and toast under the broiler.

Cut out the eyes and mouth of the squid. Remove the ink sac and internal bone. Cut off the tough points on the tentacles. Rub off the skin and wash under running water until white. Cut off the tentacles, taking care not to damage the body, and chop them finely with the garlic and parsley. Add the bread crumbs, salt, pepper and a dash olive oil. Mix the ingredients together and fill the bodies with this mixture. Sew the bodies closed with white thread. Sauté the squid in a large skillet with the ¼ cup oil, turning to brown them evenly. Season with salt and pepper, sprinkle with a little oil and pour the white wine over them. Cover the skillet, reduce the heat to very low and cook no longer than 25 minutes. When the flesh is very tender, serve the stuffed squid with slices of toasted polenta.

* Make the polenta according to the recipe on page 11. Slice in desired shapes and toast under the broiler.

BROILED CRAYFISH

BROILED SEA TROUT

(Gamberoni alla Griglia)   **Serves 6 to 8**

30 large crayfish
¼ cup olive oil
   salt and pepper

2 cloves garlic, chopped
   chopped parsley
   lemon wedges

(Volpina alla Griglia)   **Serves 6**

3 sea trout (about 1½ pounds each)
   lemon slices

   salt and pepper
   lemon wedges

Cut the pincers from the crayfish, shell the tails and wash them. Dry them with paper toweling. Soak them for 1 hour in oil, salt and pepper. Heat a broiling rack until it is very hot. Drain the oil from the crayfish and skewer them. Put them on the broiling rack and reduce the heat immediately. Cook the crayfish for about 15 minutes, turning at mid-point to brown them evenly. Arrange the crayfish on a warm serving dish. Serve hot, seasoned with oil, chopped garlic and chopped parsley. Garnish with lemon wedges.

(Dog fish, used in the original recipe, is unavailable in the United States. It is cooked in the same fashion as sea trout.)

Wash the fish and dry them well. Rub them with the lemon slices. Season with salt and pepper. Clean the broiling rack well and oil it. Heat until it is blazing hot before putting the fish on it about 6 inches from the heat. Reduce the heat immediately. Cook for about 5 minutes on the first side or until it is golden brown. Turn and cook for about 8 minutes on the other side or until the flesh flakes easily with a fork. When the fish are done, arrange them on a serving dish, garnished with wedges of lemon.

SOLE IN WHITE WINE	POACHED BASS

(Sogliola al Vino Bianco)   Serves 6

6 sole (about 1 pound each)	¼ cup dry white wine
6 tablespoons flour	juice of 1 lemon
salt and pepper	3 tablespoons dry marsala
6 sage leaves	1 tablespoon hot mustard
7 tablespoons butter	lemon wedges

(Branzino Bollito)   Serves 6

10 cups water	1 peppercorn, crushed
2 cups dry white wine	salt
¼ cup vinegar	1 striped bass (about 6 pounds)
1 lemon	½ lemon
1 carrot, finely chopped	mayonnaise (page 211)
1 onion, finely chopped	olive oil
½ celeriac, finely chopped	pepper
1 bay leaf	lemon juice

(The term "sole" in the United States refers to any member of the flounder family, any of which may be substituted for genuine sole, which is expensive and only obtainable frozen.)

Clean and skin the sole. Wash in water and a little lemon juice and dry thoroughly. Coat them lightly with flour and season with salt, pepper and the sage leaves. Melt the butter in a large skillet and sauté the fish, turning once, until both sides are evenly browned. Pour the white wine, marsala and remaining lemon juice over the fish. Stir the hot mustard into the sauce to dissolve it. Let the sauce thicken. Taste for seasoning, then remove the fish from the heat. Arrange the pieces of sole on a warm serving dish. Garnish with lemon wedges and serve immediately.

Prepare a court bouillon in a fish poacher with the water, wine, vinegar, lemon, vegetables, bay leaf, peppercorn and salt. Boil slowly for 30 minutes, skimming carefully. Cool. Wash and dry the fish. Rub it with half a lemon to prevent the skin from coming off during cooking. (If you do not have a fish poacher, wrap the bass in cheesecloth and poach on a rack in a roasting pan. Allow the cheesecloth to hang over the ends of the pan.) Put the bass into the cooled court bouillon. Bring it to a boil, reduce the heat and cook very slowly for about 35 minutes (6 minutes per pound) or until the flesh flakes easily with a fork. Remove from the heat but allow the bass to stand in the liquid for 5 minutes. Drain the fish on a rack, then place it on an oval platter. Serve accompanied with a dish of mayonnaise and a dish of oil, pepper and lemon juice lightly beaten with a fork.

BAKED STUFFED MUSSELS

GRILLED SHRIMP

(Cozze al Forno)   Serves 6

3¼ pounds mussels	2 cloves garlic, chopped
¼ cup olive oil	salt and pepper
1 cup dry bread crumbs	lemons, cut into basket-shapes
½ cup chopped parsley	

(Scampi Giganti ai Ferri)   Serves 6

36 jumbo shrimp (about 3 pounds)	chopped parsley
salt and pepper	lemon juice
¾ cup olive oil	

Wash, scrub and "beard" the mussels. Cook them in a large skillet with the oil over high heat, shaking the pan until the shells open. Reserve the mussel liquor. Discard the empty half shells and place the ones containing the mussels on an oven-proof dish. Mix the bread crumbs, parsley, garlic, salt and pepper together. Put 1 teaspoon on each mussel and sprinkle with a little oil. Strain the liquid in which the mussels were opened through a damp cheesecloth. Add a few tablespoons of this liquid to the dish of mussels and put it into a preheated 450° F. oven for about 10 minutes. If not yet browned, put under the broiler for a minute. Serve immediately garnished with lemons cut into the shape of baskets.

Shell the shrimp leaving the tails intact, and devein. Cut along the back and half-open them. Season with salt, pepper and the oil. Heat the broiler for about 10 minutes until it is very hot. Add the shrimp and reduce the heat immediately. Cook them for 5 minutes, turning several times to brown evenly without burning. Serve immediately, sprinkled with a dash olive oil, the chopped parsley and a few drops of lemon juice.

BAKED PILCHARD

(Alici in Tortiera) **Serves 6**

3 stale rolls	½ cup grated Parmesan cheese
1 cup milk	salt and pepper
2¾ pounds pilchard or infant alewives	1 egg, beaten
½ cup olive oil	small tomato wedges
½ teaspoon basil	lemon slices

(The Italians use fresh anchovies in this recipe, for which there is no substitute. Pilchard and infant alewives may be cooked in this fashion, however.)

Soak the stale rolls in the milk. Wash the fish and bone them. When all the milk has been absorbed, mix in the oil and basil. Add the cheese, salt and pepper, then bind the mixture with the beaten egg. Stuff the fish with this filling, taking care not to break them. Arrange the fish radially in an oiled, deep round baking pan. Sprinkle with oil, salt and pepper, then cook in a preheated 425° F. oven for up to 30 minutes. When the fish are golden brown, remove the pan from the oven. Garnish the fish with small tomato wedges and lemon slices; serve immediately. Fresh basil leaves add an attractive touch to the garnish.

MIXED SEAFOOD GRILL

(Griglia Mista) **Serves 6**

12 jumbo shrimp (about 1 pound)	lemon juice
1 sea squab (1¼ pounds)	pepper
1 sole (about ¾ pound)	¼ cup olive oil
1 sea bass (about 1 pound)	chopped parsley
salt	lemon wedges

Shell and devein the shrimp. Wash the shrimp, sea squab, sole and bass in plenty of salted water and lemon juice. Dry the fish gently and season the insides and outsides with salt and pepper. Wipe the broiling rack and heat for about 10 minutes until very hot. Skewer the shrimp and sea squab. Put the sea squab in the broiler first, as it requires more cooking than any of the other fish. Then add the bass (15 minutes total), followed by the sole (10 minutes total) and the shrimp (5 minutes total). Lower the heat when the fish become golden, and turn the skewers to brown the fish evenly. Cook for about a total of 25 minutes. Serve the hot fish seasoned with a mixture of oil, salt, chopped parsley and lemon juice. Serve immediately, garnished with lemon wedges.

ASSORTED FRIED SHELLFISH

MARINATED CRABMEAT

(Fritto Misto di Pesce)   **Serves 6 to 8**

1¼ pounds jumbo shrimp
1¼ pounds large crayfish
1¼ pounds small crayfish
    salt

lemon juice
6 tablespoons flour
   oil for frying
   lemon wedges

(Granchio di Mare in Zuppiera)   **Serves 6**

15 blue claw crabs or 1 pound
    crabmeat
    salt
    bouquet garni
    pepper
½ cup olive oil

2 cloves garlic, chopped
   chopped parsley
   lemon juice
   lemon wedges

Shell and devein the shrimp and crayfish and wash several times in salted water and a few drops of lemon juice. Dry them well with paper toweling and coat them with flour. Heat the oil in a large skillet. The large shellfish require more cooking time and less heat; the smaller ones must be fried quickly in boiling oil. Remember, therefore, to cook the shellfish in order of size. As soon as the shellfish become golden brown and crisp, remove them from the oil with a mesh ladle and drain on absorbent paper. Salt the fish when hot and serve immediately, garnished with lemon wedges.

Clean and wash the crabs. Heat a large quantity of salted water with a bouquet garni. When the water comes to a boil, plunge the crabs into it. Cover and boil 15 to 20 minutes or until the shells are red. Drain and cool. Break off the claws, crack and pick out the meat. Break off the tail and pull the upper and lower shells apart. Wash away any loose matter and remove the meat. (Reserve some shells.) Put the crabmeat in a soup tureen and season with a mixture of salt, pepper, the oil, chopped garlic, chopped parsley and a few drops of lemon juice. Marinate the crab in this sauce for at least 1 hour. Decorate the edge of the tureen with crab shells and serve the crabmeat accompanied with a variety of salads and lemon wedges.

SEA SQUAB IN WHITE WINE

BROILED TUNA STEAKS

(Coda di Rospo al Vino Bianco)   **Serves 6**

6 sea squab (about 10 ounces each)	1 teaspoon finely chopped
½ cup flour	rosemary
1 onion, finely chopped	½ cup olive oil
2 cloves garlic, finely chopped	salt and pepper
1 stalk celery, finely chopped	1 cup dry white wine
2 tablespoons finely chopped parsley	

(Tranci di Tonno ai Ferri)   **Serves 6**

2 tuna steaks (about 1¼ pounds each)	½ onion, chopped
½ cup olive oil	2 cloves garlic, chopped
salt and pepper	chopped parsley
1 bay leaf	2 tablespoons chopped capers

Wash sea squab in salted water or water with lemon juice and dry them. Dredge the fish in flour. Heat the oil in a large saucepan and gently cook the onion, garlic, celery, parsley and rosemary for a few minutes. Increase the heat and add the sea squab. Brown them quickly on both sides and season with salt and pepper. Add the white wine and transfer the pan to a preheated 325° F. oven for about 30 minutes, basting the fish occasionally with the sauce in which it is cooking. Serve the fish in a warm oven-proof dish covered with the sauce. Garnish with sprigs of rosemary.

Marinate the tuna steaks in a mixture of oil, salt, pepper, bay leaf and onion for 1 hour. Remove the tuna steaks from the marinade and place them on a very hot broiling rack that has been preheated for 10 minutes. Brown the fish, then reduce the heat. Cook evenly on both sides, brushing the slices occasionally with the remainder of the marinade for about 10 minutes, the fish should not "bleed." When the steaks are well cooked, season with a mixture of oil, chopped garlic, parsley and capers. Serve immediately.

SMELTS WITH SCRAMBLED EGGS

POACHED TROUT

(Alborelle con le Uova)   Serves 6 to 8

2¼	pounds smelts		salt
½	cup flour	10	eggs, beaten
	olive oil	3½	tablespoons butter

(Lavarello Bollito)   Serves 6

6	cups water	1	peppercorn, crushed
2	cups dry white wine		salt
1	onion, finely chopped	6	rainbow trout (about ¾ pound
1	carrot, finely chopped		each)
½	celeriac, finely chopped		pickled onions
1	bay leaf		lemon wedges
			mayonnaise (page 211)

(Alborelle, or bleak, is a very small freshwater fish unavailable in this country. We have substituted smelts in this recipe.)

Soak the smelts in ice water for 1 or 2 hours. Drain and dry them. Dust with flour. Heat the oil in a large skillet and fry the fish, shaking the pan constantly to cook evenly. Drain the fish on absorbent paper, then sprinkle with salt. Add the fried fish to the beaten eggs. Melt the butter in a large skillet, add the eggs and fish and cook over low heat, stirring with a fork, until the egg thickens. When the mixture is soft and creamy, serve it in a hot buttered dish.

Prepare a court bouillon in a fish poacher by boiling the water and wine with the vegetables, bay leaf, peppercorn and salt for 5 minutes. (If you do not have a poacher, use a roasting pan and rack.) Skim the liquid, then remove it from the heat and cool. Clean and wash the fish thoroughly. Dry them with paper toweling and dip them in lemon juice to prevent the skin from breaking during cooking. Put the fish into the poacher and simmer. When the flesh flakes easily with a fork, turn off the heat. Let the fish remain in the court bouillon for 5 minutes, then take them out and drain on a rack. Serve the hot fish decorated with carrot slices, bay leaves and parsley, and accompanied with pickled onions and lemon wedges. Serve mayonnaise on the side.

(Pesce Spada) Serves 6

2 swordfish steaks (about 2½ pounds each)	2 cloves garlic, chopped
6 tablespoons flour	½ onion, chopped
½ cup olive oil	¼ cup dry white wine
salt and pepper	juice of 1 lemon
	lemon slices

Dust the steaks with flour and put them into a large skillet. Season with oil, salt, pepper, garlic and onion, then pour in the wine and lemon juice. Seal the pan very tightly with a piece of aluminum foil tied around the top; cover with the lid. Put the skillet into a preheated 425° F. oven for about 30 minutes. The fish will cook in its own steam with its seasonings. When it is ready, serve from an oven-proof dish, garnished with lemon slices.

(Gamberi alle Erbe Aromatiche) Serves 6

water to cover crayfish	½ bay leaf
1 onion, chopped	1 peppercorn, crushed
1 carrot, chopped	salt
1 celeriac, chopped	24 freshwater crayfish

For the sauce

¼ cup olive oil	3 cloves garlic, crushed
2 tablespoons flour	⅓ teaspoon paprika
salt	⅓ teaspoon nutmeg
chopped parsley	⅓ teaspoon black pepper

Prepare a court bouillon by boiling water with the vegetables, ½ bay leaf, peppercorn and salt for 5 minutes. Cool. Wash the crayfish well, peel them and dry them with a cloth. Put them into the court bouillon and bring to a boil. Cook for 5 minutes then drain; reserve 1 cup court bouillon. **To prepare the sauce:** Heat the oil in a saucepan, stir in the flour with a wooden spoon and cook for a few minutes. Add the reserved court bouillon in which the crayfish were cooked and beat the mixture with a wire whisk until it is light, smooth and creamy. Season with salt, the parsley, garlic, paprika, nutmeg and black pepper. Mix once more and pour the sauce into a dish. Serve the sauce with the boiled crayfish.

(Tartine di Gamberetti)   Serves 6

4 tablespoons butter	1½ pounds frozen crayfish
2 tablespoons flour	few slices bread
1 cup clear stock	chopped parsley
salt	

(Salmerino Cotto nel Pane)   Serves 6

6 brook trout (about ¾ pound each)	salt and pepper
½ cup olive oil	22 cups (5 pounds plus 2 cups)
¼ cup rum	flour
3 cloves garlic, crushed	4 cups water
1 tablespoon fennel seeds	2 eggs, beaten
10 sage leaves	mayonnaise (page 211)
chopped parsley	oil and vinegar

Prepare a thick béchamel sauce by creaming together the butter and flour. Heat them in a saucepan and when the butter becomes golden brown, pour in the stock; season with salt. Prepare the shrimp according to the instructions on the package. Cut the bread very accurately into 2-inch squares. Spread each square with the béchamel sauce and top with the shrimp. Arrange the squares on an oven-proof dish and put them into a preheated 425° F. oven for 5 minutes. Remove from the oven and spinkle with chopped parsley. A simpler canapé can be prepared by spreading the bread with mayonnaise and topping with the boiled shrimp. Serve with lettuce, tomato wedges, quarters of hard cooked egg, lemon slices and parsley, as shown in the photograph.

Clean, wash and dry trout. Marinate for 3 hours in a mixture of the oil, rum, garlic, fennel seeds, sage leaves, parsley, salt and pepper. Mix the flour and water together until the dough is smooth. Roll out the dough to a thickness of ¼ inch and cut the pastry into six rectangles. Remove the fish from the marinade and drain them. Place a fish in the middle of each rectangle and wrap it up in such a way as to show its outline. Using a knife and a spoon, sculpt the shape of the head, fins, scales and tail. Brush the surface of the dough with the beaten eggs. Insert a few toothpicks into the dough to allow steam to escape. Flour a baking sheet and place the fish on it. Cook in a preheated 425° F. oven for 30 minutes. Serve the fish accompanied with mayonnaise and a sauce made from oil, vinegar, salt and pepper.

BROILED CARP

TROUT IN WHITE WINE

(Carpione ai Ferri)   **Serves 6**

3 carp (about 1¼ pounds each)   3 tablespoons olive oil
  lemon slices   lemon juice
  salt and pepper   lemon wedges

(Trota al Vino Bianco)   **Serves 6**

3 trout (about 1¾ pounds each)   salt and pepper
  lemon slices   6 sage leaves
¼ cup flour   ½ cup dry white wine
7 tablespoons butter   lemon wedges

Carp have delicate flesh and skin, so choose fresh fish and handle them gently. Clean, wash and dry the fish. Rub the skin gently with slices of lemon, season the inside of each with salt and pepper and lay the fish on a clean, very hot broiling rack. Reduce the heat, immediately. Turn the carp when they are brown and remove from the heat when the flesh is soft to the touch. Sprinkle them with the oil and lemon juice. Arrange the fish on a serving dish decorated with a variety of salad greens and tomato slices. Garnish with lemon wedges. Serve the carp very hot.

Clean the trout carefully, as the skin and flesh are very soft. Wash and dry them. Rub the skin gently with lemon slices to prevent it from splitting; dust with flour. Melt the butter in a large skillet until it foams, then reduce the heat, add the trout and brown gently on both sides. Sprinkle with salt and pepper and add the sage leaves. Pour in the white wine and put the pan into a preheated 425° F. oven immediately. When the flesh flakes easily, remove the fish from the pan and drain. Arrange the trout on a serving dish decorated with salad greens and ripe tomatoes. Garnish with lemon wedges.

BAKED STUFFED CARP

(Tinca Ripiena al Forno)   Serves 6

1 carp (about 4 pounds)
salt
chopped parsley
2 cloves garlic, chopped
2½ cups soft bread crumbs
¾ cup grated Parmesan cheese
3 eggs

3 sage leaves
½ bay leaf
pepper
dry bread crumbs
¼ cup olive oil
½ cup dry white wine

Scald the carp in boiling salted water and skin it. Wash in cold water. Mix together the parsley, garlic, soft bread crumbs, Parmesan cheese, eggs, sage leaves, bay leaf and pepper; stuff the fish with this mixture. Press the opening closed with your fingers and coat the fish in dry bread crumbs. Put the stuffed fish in an oven-proof dish, add the oil and season with salt and pepper. Put the fish into a preheated 350° F. oven to bake for 1 hour, basting it first with the white wine, then with its own juices. This dish goes well with slices of hot polenta (cornmeal mush).

FRIED EELS

(Anguilla Dorata)   Serves 6

2 eels (about 1¾ pounds each)
salt and pepper
3 eggs, beaten
6 tablespoons dry bread crumbs

6 tablespoons grated Parmesan
cheese
½ cup olive oil
lemon wedges

Cut the heads off the eels, skin them, gut them and cut into 2-inch slices. Rinse well under running water and dry. Add salt and pepper to the beaten eggs. Dip the pieces of eel into the egg mixture, then coat them with a mixture of bread crumbs and Parmesan cheese. Heat the oil in a large skillet until it sizzles, then fry the eel slices quickly. When the slices are golden brown, remove them with a slotted spoon and drain them on absorbent paper. Salt them while still hot. Prepare a bed of salad greens on a serving dish, then place the slices of eel on top. Serve the dish with lemon wedges and with sprigs of sage and rosemary standing in sectioned lemons and with tomatoes cut to form tiny baskets.

FISH SOUP

STEWED SQUID WITH PEAS

Photo Findus

Photo Findus

(Zuppa di Pesce)   **Serves 6**

3 pounds mixed fish (eel, mullet, octo-
    pus, squid, mussels)
8 cups water
2 carrots
2 stalks celery
1 bay leaf
   salt and pepper

1 onion, finely chopped
3 cloves garlic
4 anchovy fillets, finely chopped
¾ pound tomatoes, peeled
6 tablespoons olive oil
6 slices stale bread
   chopped parsley

(Seppie in Umido con Piselli)   **Serves 6**

2¾ pounds cleaned or frozen squid
6 tablespoons olive oil
1 clove garlic
   salt and pepper
½ cup dry white wine
6 anchovy fillets, very finely chopped

¾ pound tomatoes, peeled and put
    through a food mill
2 cups shelled peas
   chopped parsley

Clean and wash the fish, then cut them into pieces. Remove the heads, tails, bones and shells and use them to make the fish stock with the water, carrots, celery, bay leaf, salt and pepper. Put the onion, 2 cloves of the garlic and the anchovies into a deep pan with the oil to brown. Then add all the fish, (except the octopus and squid, if using them—they should be added to the pan 5 minutes before adding the other fish). Stir in the tomatoes and stock. Boil the soup gently for 15 minutes. Taste for seasoning. Rub the slices of bread with the remaining garlic, sprinkle with a few drops of olive oil and toast lightly in the oven. Put a slice of bread in each plate and pour the hot soup over it. Sprinkle with a little chopped parsley. Serve immediately.

Cut the squid into strips. Put the oil and garlic into a pan and heat. When the garlic becomes golden, add the squid to the pan and season with salt and pepper. Add the wine and let the mixture simmer for a few minutes. Then add the anchovy fillets, the puréed tomatoes and enough water to cover the squid. Cover and cook for about 20 minutes, then add the peas. When the peas and squid are tender, remove the pan from the heat. Garnish with chopped parsley just before serving.

Eggs

The use of eggs in Italian cookery dates back to ancient times. In Imperial Rome the eggs of many different species of bird were used. This may have been to compensate for a lack of variety in cooking methods. Today we generally use hens' eggs but tradition and imagination have provided us with an extensive range of recipes. The recipes given in this chapter set out to express the basic ideas for cooking eggs but many other variations can be introduced to suit the taste and creative imagination of those preparing them

SHIRRED EGGS

SCRAMBLED EGGS WITH TOMATO

(Uova al Burro) Serves 1

1 tablespoon butter salt and pepper
2 eggs

(Uova Strapazzate al Pomodoro) Serves 1

1 tablespoon butter salt and pepper
2 eggs 1 tablespoon heavy cream
2 tablespoons tomato sauce

Melt half of the butter in an earthenware dish. Break the eggs into a dish and slide them into the melted butter, taking care not to break the yolks. Heat the other half of the butter until it is golden, then pour it onto the whites of the eggs. Put the eggs into a preheated 325° F. oven for 15 to 18 minutes. When they are set, season with salt and pepper. Serve them immediately from the dish in which they were cooked.

Melt half of the butter in a flame-proof dish; do not let it brown. Break the eggs into a bowl, whip them with a fork and add the tomato sauce, salt and pepper. As soon as the butter is foaming, pour the eggs and tomato sauce into the dish. Stir the mixture towards the center of the dish. Add the cream and the remaining butter. When the mixture is set but still soft and creamy remove from the heat and serve at once.

HARD COOKED EGGS	POACHED EGGS

(Uova Sode)

eggs

oil

salt and pepper

(Uova Affogate o in Camicia) Serves 1

2 quarts water

juice of 1 lemon

½ cup white vinegar

2 eggs

Soak the eggs in cold water. Put some water in a wide, shallow pan and when it begins to simmer, place the eggs carefully on the bottom of the pan with a spoon. Let the eggs simmer for 8 minutes, then remove them. Put them in cold water. The shells can now be removed easily. Cut the eggs in half lengthwise and season them with some oil, salt and pepper. Serve the eggs on a decorated dish.

Boil the water, lemon juice and vinegar in a wide, shallow pan. Break the first egg into a cup. When the water begins to simmer gently, slip the egg into the water. Remove the pan from the heat and wait for the white to set and the yolk to be the desired doneness before gently removing the egg with a slotted spoon. Drain the egg on a clean towel and trim the edge with a knife or a round cutter. Repeat this procedure with the other egg. When they are both cooked, serve them on lettuce leaves.

EGGS WITH CROUTONS AND POTATO　　PRAIRIE OYSTERS

(Uova con Crostini e Patate)　　　　　　　　　**Serves 1**

12 *small cubes bread*
12 *tiny cubes cold, boiled potato*
 3 *tablespoons butter*

2 *eggs*
　salt and pepper

(Uova all'Ostrica)

egg yolks
salt and pepper

few drops lemon juice
lemon wedges

Brown the cubed bread and potato with 2 tablespoons of butter in a small saucepan. Beat the eggs in a bowl; add salt, pepper and the bread and potato cubes. Melt the remaining butter slowly in a flame-proof dish, then pour in the egg mixture. Stir constantly until the mixture is set but still soft and creamy. Serve immediately.

Put the yolks from the raw eggs into special porcelain or metal spoons designed for "prairie oysters." Season the yolks with a little salt, a lot of pepper and a few drops of lemon juice. Serve these "prairie oysters" with lemon wedges.

(Uova alla Fontina)   Serves 1

1 tablespoon butter
2 eggs
   salt and pepper

2 thin slices ham
2 thin slices fontina cheese
2 tablespoons white wine

(Uova Farcite)   Serves 6

6 eggs
3 anchovy fillets
2 ounces canned tuna fish in oil

½ teaspoon hot mustard
2 teaspoons mayonnaise

Heat the butter in a small oven-proof dish. Break the eggs into a saucer and then slide them gently into the center of the oven-proof dish without breaking the yolks. Season the eggs with salt and pepper. Cover each yolk with a thin slice of ham and a slice of fontina cheese. Pour the white wine over the cheese. Put the dish into a preheated 350° F. oven until the eggs have set, the cheese melted and the wine evaporated. Serve immediately.

Put the eggs into a saucepan, cover them with cold water and bring to a boil. Boil gently for 8 to 9 minutes. Put the eggs into cold water, shell them and cut them in half lengthwise. Remove the hard cooked yolks and purée them through a food mill with the anchovies and tuna fish. (Reserve the hollowed-out egg whites.) Mix this well and add the mustard and mayonnaise. Fit a decorator's bag with a star tube and fill the bag with the mixture. Pipe a rose-shaped swirl into the whites of the eggs. This dish is attractive served on a bed of salad greens covered with grated carrot. Garnish with wedges of tomato and strips of yellow pepper.

RED PEPPER OMELETTE   EGGS, RUSSIAN STYLE

(Omelette con Peperoni)   Serves 1

¼ onion, chopped
2 tablespoons olive oil
2 red peppers, cut into strips

2 eggs
   salt and pepper
1 tablespoon butter

(Uova alla Russa)   Serves 6

6 eggs
¼ cup thick mayonnaise
1 tablespoon caviar

12 thin slices smoked salmon
    butter

Sauté the chopped onion in the oil over low heat. Add the peppers, cover the saucepan and continue to cook slowly. Break the eggs into a bowl, season them with salt and pepper and beat with a fork. Melt the butter in an omelette pan and when it covers the bottom of the pan, pour in the eggs. Keep the heat high, stir the eggs and lower the heat as soon as they begin to set. Shake the pan and run a fork around the edge of the omelette to prevent it from sticking to the pan. Stir continuously, keeping the consistency of the omelette creamy. Put two-thirds of the cooked peppers in the middle, then fold the edge of the omelette towards the middle into the usual long, narrow omelette shape. Slip it onto a serving dish and serve immediately with the rest of the peppers on top.

Put the eggs in a saucepan, cover them with cold water and bring to a boil. Cook the eggs for about 10 minutes, until they are hard cooked. Place them in cold water, shell them and cut them in half lengthwise. Put the mayonnaise into a decorator's bag fitted with a notched tip. Decorate the half eggs with a thin strip of mayonnaise. Sprinkle a little caviar over the mayonnaise. Roll the slices of salmon into cones, keeping one end more closed than the other. The cone will retain its shape better if the inside is lightly spread with butter, then pressed down with the fingers. Insert the tube into the open end of the salmon horns and decorate with little rosettes of mayonnaise. This sophisticated antipasto should be attractively served on a bed of lettuce leaves, garnished with slices of lemon and tomato. Decorate the center of the dish with a yellow flower.

SPINACH and TOMATO OMELETTE

TRUFFLE and FONTINA CHEESE OMELETTE

(Tortino di Spinaci e Pomodoro)   **Serves 1**

¼ pound spinach
¼ ·onion, chopped
 6 tablespoons olive oil
    salt and pepper

¼ cup peeled, chopped tomatoes
 2 eggs
 1 tablespoon butter
    tomato sauce

(Tortino con Tartufi e Fontina)   **Serves 1**

 2 eggs
    salt and pepper
¼ cup finely diced fontina cheese

 1 tablespoon butter
 1 canned truffle

Remove the stems from the spinach and wash it in plenty of water. Sauté the onion lightly in the oil and add the spinach. Season with salt and pepper, add a few pieces of tomato and cover to let the spinach steam. Break the eggs into a dish and beat them with a fork; add salt and pepper and the cooked spinach. Melt the butter in a pan and when it is frothy, add the egg and spinach mixture. As soon as it begins to set, shake the pan to prevent the omelette from sticking. Using an egg turner, turn the omelette to cook the other side. Slip it onto a serving dish and pour some previously prepared tomato sauce onto the center of the omelette and around the sides.

Put the eggs in a bowl and beat with a fork. Season with salt and pepper and add the fontina cheese. Melt the butter in a flame-proof dish; do not let it become brown. Pour the eggs and cheese into the hot butter, stirring continuously to prevent the mixture from becoming too thick. When the mixture is set but still creamy, remove it from the heat. Slice the truffle over the egg mixture with a truffle cutter. Serve the dish piping hot.

It has been said that Italian cooking does not make use of sauces, but this is not quite true. Although Italians do not use the great international sauces, they make good use of their own ones, which have strong flavors. Italian sauces do not accompany the food as harmonious partners but interpret it and make it alive, pouring on it all the warmth of a Mediterranean climate. Lately however, international sauces, especially French ones, have gained a foothold in Italian cooking. Other genuine Italian traditional sauces, such as tomato, basil and anchovy, are basic sauces which, owing to their wide range, can be varied to satisfy the most sophisticated palate.

MAYONNAISE

(Salsa Maionese) **Serves 6**

4 egg yolks
  juice of 1 lemon
2 cups peanut oil

salt and white pepper
2 tablespoons vinegar, heated

Put the egg yolks and a little of the lemon juice into a narrow-bottomed bowl. Stir steadily and continuously with a wooden spoon or a small whisk. Add half of the oil drop by drop. As soon as the mayonnaise begins to thicken, add drops of lemon juice to prevent it from becoming too thick. Season it with salt and pepper and mix in the other half of the oil in a gentle trickle, stirring continuously. As a finishing touch, add the hot vinegar, whipping vigorously to blend it well into the sauce. The addition of vinegar ensures that the sauce will not separate and will be smooth and fine in texture.

BÉCHAMEL SAUCE

(Salsa Besciamella) **Serves 6**

4 tablespoons butter
½ cup flour
1 quart milk, boiling
  salt
  pinch white pepper

pinch nutmeg
1 tiny onion
1 sprig thyme
1 bay leaf

Melt the butter in a saucepan over a low heat. Mix in the flour and cook it in the butter until it is golden, stirring continuously with a wooden spoon. Thin the mixture by adding boiling milk. Simmer the sauce for about 20 minutes, stirring constantly until it is creamy, velvety and smooth in texture. Add the salt, pepper, nutmeg and onion and the thyme and bay leaf (tied together for removal when the sauce is ready). If any lumps appear during the cooking, put the sauce through a sieve. Dot the surface of the sauce with a few pieces of butter to prevent a skin from forming. This sauce can be used as an accompaniment or to thicken or enrich various dishes.

TARTAR SAUCE

RED PEPPER SAUCE

(Salsa alla Tatara) Serves 6

2 egg yolks
2 hard cooked egg yolks
2 cups peanut oil
2 tablespoons vinegar
  juice of 1 lemon
  salt

½ onion, finely chopped
1 clove garlic, finely chopped
½ green pepper, finely chopped
1 tablespoon finely chopped
  capers
¼ cup finely chopped parsley

(Salsa al Peperoncino) Serves 6

4 egg yolks
2 cups sunflower-seed oil
  juice of 1 lemon

salt
2 teaspoons chili powder

To prepare tartar sauce, half of the egg yolks must be raw and half hard cooked. Otherwise the method is the same as for mayonnaise. Mix the 2 raw egg yolks and the 2 hard cooked yolks in a bowl. Blend them together with a wooden spoon until they form a smooth paste. Add the oil in drops until the sauce thickens, then pour the remaining oil into the sauce in a smooth trickle. Add the vinegar and lemon juice to dilute the mixture, then season it with salt. Now add the finely chopped onion, garlic, green pepper, capers and parsley. Mix slowly and pour into a dish. This tasty sauce can be used as an accompaniment to many dishes and is particularly good with fish.

Put the egg yolks in a bowl, blend them together with a wooden spoon or a small whisk, then whip them steadily. Add half of the oil in drops until the sauce thickens. Dilute with a little lemon juice and season with salt. Add the other half of the oil in a trickle while continuing to beat the sauce. Lastly, add the chili powder to the mayonnaise.

GREEN SAUCE

TOMATO SAUCE

(Salsa Verde)   **Serves 6**

½ pound parsley
4 anchovies in brine
  juice of ½ lemon
1 green pepper
1 clove garlic (inner bud removed)

¼ onion, chopped
1 bottle (2½ ounces) capers,
  drained and chopped
½ cup olive oil
  salt

(Salsa di Pomodoro)   **Serves 6**

1 pound tomatoes, peeled and chopped
  salt and pepper
1 small carrot, chopped
1 small onion, chopped
1 stalk celery, chopped

3 basil leaves, chopped
½ clove garlic, chopped
½ cup olive oil
1 teaspoon sugar

Choose some fresh garden parsley with tiny, aromatic leaves and wash it well. Scrape the salt from the anchovies, wash them with lemon juice and remove any bones. Scorch the pepper over a gas flame and peel. Cut the pepper, wash out the seeds, rinse it under running water and cut it into strips. Put the parsley, anchovies, strips of pepper, garlic, onion and capers into a vegetable grinder to produce a very finely chopped mixture. Dilute the mixture with olive oil and lemon juice. Taste the sauce for salt. Serve in a sauce dish as an accompaniment to main courses and vegetables.

Season the chopped tomatoes lightly with salt and pepper and drain. Cook the vegetables, basil and garlic in 2 tablespoons of the oil over low heat for a few minutes. Add the tomatoes, bring to a boil and cook over medium heat to bring out the full flavor. When the vegetables are cooked and the tomatoes are becoming dry, put the mixture through a food mill. If necessary, put the sauce back over the heat to thicken. Taste the sauce for salt; add the remaining oil and the sugar to counteract the acidity of the tomatoes. Sieve the sauce and serve it in a sauce dish.

BASIL SAUCE

PEPPERY VERONA SAUCE

(Salsa al Basilico)   Serves 6

½ pound basil
2 cloves garlic (inner buds removed)
½ cup pine nuts

¾ cup grated Romano cheese
   salt and pepper
½ cup olive oil

(Salsa "Pearà"—Peperata)   Serves 6

2 ounces beef marrow
3 tablespoons butter
5 cups fresh bread crumbs
1 quart (approximately) clear stock,
   boiling

½ cup grated Parmesan cheese
   salt
   freshly ground black pepper

Choose fresh, fragrant garden basil. Wash the basil and chop it with the garlic and pine nuts. Add the grated Romano cheese, salt and pepper. Dilute the mixture with the olive oil and serve it in an elegant sauce dish.

Melt the marrow and butter in an earthenware dish. Add the bread crumbs, preferably from an unsalted white loaf. Stir with a wooden spoon until the bread has absorbed the marrow and butter. Add ladlefuls of boiling clear stock until the sauce has a creamy texture. Cook very slowly for a long time, stirring occasionally, until the sauce is very thick. Just before serving, add the grated Parmesan cheese, salt if necessary and plenty of freshly ground black pepper. Serve the sauce very hot. This thick sauce should be served as an accompaniment to boiled meats.

Vinegar Horseradish Sauce Serves 6

(Salsa al Cren all'Aceto)

1 horseradish (about 5 ounces)	pinch salt
1½ cups fresh bread crumbs	pinch sugar
milk	½ cup white vinegar

(Salsa ai Capperi e Acciuga) Serves 6

2 ounces anchovy fillets in salt	2 bottles (2½ ounces each)
1 tablespoon chopped onion	capers drained and chopped
1 tablespoon butter	dash vinegar
	1½ tablespoons butter, creamed

Scrape, wash and grate the horseradish. Soak the bread crumbs in milk, then squeeze out the excess liquid. Put the horseradish pulp into a sauce dish, add the bread crumbs, salt and sugar. Mix well and dilute with white vinegar. Serve the sauce with boiled meats.

Scrape the salt from the anchovies, bone and chop. Brown the chopped onion gently over low heat with the butter. Remove the saucepan from the heat and add the chopped anchovies and capers. Add the vinegar and mix the creamed butter into the sauce.

Creamed Horseradish Sauce

(Salsa al Cren alla Panna) Serves 6

1 horseradish (about 5 ounces)	pinch sugar
pinch salt	½ cup heavy cream

Scrape, wash and grate the horseradish. Collect the moist pulp in a sauce dish and add the salt and sugar to it. Whip the cream lightly, but not to a peak, and mix this gently into the horseradish. Serve as an accompaniment to antipasto or cold fish and cold meats.

BLACK OLIVE SAUCE

(Salsa alle Olive)   Serves 6

½ onion, sliced
½ cup olive oil
1 cup pitted black olives, finely chopped
¼ cup tomatoes, peeled, seeded and chopped
salt and pepper

Brown the onion in a small oven-proof dish with the oil. Add the chopped olives and the tomatoes to the onion. Cook the sauce over medium heat for 10 minutes, then add salt and pepper. Serve in a sauce dish.

PICKLED GREEN PEPPER SAUCE

(Salsa ai Peperoni)   Serves 6

½ pound pickled green peppers
1¼ cups coarsely grated Parmesan cheese
pinch dry mustard
salt
½ cup olive oil

Remove the seeds from the pickled peppers and chop finely. Mix the cheese with the peppers. Add the mustard; season with salt if necessary and dilute the sauce with the olive oil. Pour the sauce into a shallow dish decorated with pieces of cucumber, whole pickled peppers and pickled onions. This sauce is excellent served with boiled meats.

It can be said that the science of food technology began when the French rural economist Parmentier (1737-1813) carried out a systematic investigation into the cultivation of the potato and the most practical methods of its use in cookery. At about the same time the tomato, which was introduced into Europe from America, lost its place as an exotic garden plant and gained recognition as the succulent fruit which has had such success in both Italian and international cookery. There are a few vegetables mentioned here which are not readily available in the United States and indeed, in the case of red chicory, not sold here. Ordinary chicory may be used instead, or, if the leaves are being used for decoration, any suitable alternative which appeals may be used. All the recipes collected in this section show what can be achieved with the simplest of ingredients: those in the vegetable garden. The discovery of the importance of vitamins has caused vegetables to play a greater role in cooking. At the same time, raw vegetables are being used increasingly in a great variety of salad dishes. These dishes brighten a meal, their gay colors providing a visual appeal which should overcome the poorest of appetites.

(Insalata Mista)   Serves 6

¼ pound romaine
¼ pound curly endive
¼ pound red cabbage
    salt
½ cucumber, peeled and thinly sliced
¼ pound tomatoes, sliced
¼ pound carrots, shredded
¼ cup olive oil

few drops herb vinegar
    pepper
1 bottle (2¼ ounces) capers,
    drained and chopped
4 anchovy fillets, chopped
½ onion, chopped
1 clove garlic, chopped

(Insalata in Pinzimonio)   Serves 6

1 bunch celery, separated
1 head fennel, quartered
2 yellow peppers, cut in strips
2 heads romaine, separated
1 carrot, cut in strips

1 bunch radishes
1 celeriac, cut in strips
1 cup olive oil
¼ cup herb vinegar
    salt and pepper

Wash the romaine, curly endive and cabbage, removing the stems and any wilted leaves. Dry with paper toweling. Chop the romaine and curly endive in pieces; separate the cabbage leaves and chop. Salt the cucumber and put into a strainer to drain off the excess water. Arrange these vegetables and the tomatoes and carrots in separate pottery bowls with a floral design on them. Serve the mixed vegetable salad with a sauce made by blending together the oil, vinegar, salt and pepper, capers, anchovies, onion and garlic.

All these vegetables are served with a sauce made by whipping together the olive oil, herb vinegar, salt and pepper. This pinzimonio sauce should be poured into six tiny dishes, one for each guest. The edible part of each vegetable should be dipped in the sauce and eaten by hand.

HERRING, ONION AND PEPPER SALAD RUGOLA

(Peperoni con Aringhe e Cipolla)

3 yellow peppers	¼ cup olive oil
1 onion, finely sliced	juice of ½ lemon
6 ounces smoked herring fillets,	pepper
chopped	1 tablespoon anchovy paste

(Insalata di Lattughella)   **Serves 6**

1 pound rugola lettuce	2 anchovies, chopped
1 tablespoon vinegar	salt and pepper
1 tablespoon lemon juice	5 tablespoons olive oil
1 clove garlic (inner bud removed),	
chopped	

Scorch the peppers over a gas flame and peel. Cut them in half and remove the seeds and white bits from the inside. Soak the peppers in cold water. Drain, dry and cut them into lengthwise strips. Mix the peppers, onion and herring together, then add the olive oil, lemon juice, a little pepper and the anchovy paste. Serve the salad in a rustic earthenware dish.

Wash the rugola, discarding any bruised or wilted leaves. Soak the tender leaves in plenty of water and wrap them in a linen cloth to dry; do not squeeze them. Add the vinegar and lemon juice to the garlic and anchovies, then season with a little salt and a dash of pepper. Season the lettuce with this dressing, mix the oil in gently and serve.

CARROT SALAD WITH ANCHOVIES

CELERIAC WITH MAYONNAISE

(Carote all'Acciuga)　　　　　　　　**Serves 6**

    3 anchovies in salt
       lemon slices
    ½ onion
    3 tablespoons olive oil

    1 tablespoon vinegar
       lemon juice
       pepper
    5 to 6 carrots, grated

(Sedano alla Maionese)　　　　　　　　**Serves 6**

    3 celeriac
       salt

       juice of 1 lemon
    ½ cup mayonnaise (page 211)

Scrape the salt from the anchovies, clean them with slices of lemon and bone. Chop them with the onion to a paste. Mix this in a bowl with the oil, vinegar, lemon juice and pepper. Heap the grated carrots in a salad bowl lined with lettuce leaves; pour the dressing over the carrots.

Peel the celeriac and cut into julienne. Put the strips in a bowl, salt them and soak them in the lemon juice to prevent them from turning black. Prepare the mayonnaise and add it to the celeriac in spoonfuls, mixing it in slowly so that the sauce will remain light. Arrange the celeriac and mayonnaise in an oval dish. Serve as an antipasto or as an accompaniment to a cold supper dish.

GREEN PEAS WITH MAYONNAISE

GRILLED RED CHICORY

(Piselli alla Maionese)   Serves 6

3 pounds peas   2 quarts water
    salt   ½ cup mayonnaise (page 211)

(Radicchio Rosso ai Ferri)   Serves 6

12 small curly endive   salt and pepper
¼ cup olive oil

Shell the peas and wash them; boil them briskly for about 15 minutes in the salted water. When they are cooked, drain them and run some cold water over them to retain their green color. Moisten the peas with the freshly prepared mayonnaise, mixing it in gently to keep the sauce light. Arrange the peas and mayonnaise in a dish. Serve as an accompaniment to a cold supper dish.

(Red chicory is not available in the United States, but curly endive may be substituted.)

Choose firm, tightly closed plants. Clean and wash them carefully. Scrape the root and cut the endive in half lengthwise. Shake the water from the plants and dry them thoroughly in a linen cloth, being careful not to damage the leaves. Mix together the oil, salt and pepper and baste the leaves with this mixture. Put endive on a grill and cook over hot charcoal, turning occasionally to roast thoroughly on all sides. Serve hot as an accompaniment to spit-cooked game.

PARSLIED ARTICHOKE HEARTS

ARTICHOKES, ROMAN STYLE

(Fondi di Carciofi Trifolati)   **Serves 6**

12 artichoke hearts
    juice of 1 lemon
6 tablespoons olive oil
3 cloves garlic

¼ cup flour
    salt and pepper
½ cup water or clear stock
    chopped parsley

(Carciofi alla Romana)   **Serves 6**

12 small artichokes
    lemon slices
    chopped mint
2 cloves garlic, chopped

¾ cups dry bread crumbs
    salt and pepper
½ cup olive oil
1 cup water

Use canned, medium-sized, tender artichoke hearts. Put them in water and lemon juice to keep them white until they are cooked. Heat the oil in a skillet and sauté the garlic until golden brown; remove and discard. Flour the artichoke hearts and place them in the skillet. Sauté them until golden brown, season them with salt and pepper, add some water or clear stock, cover the pan and cook slowly. Just before removing them from the heat add salt to prevent them from becoming black. When the artichoke hearts are tender, arrange them in an oval oven-proof dish. Sprinkle with some of their own juices and garnish with chopped parsley.

Remove the outer leaves from the artichokes, cut away the hard, sinewy part from the inside leaves and cut the tips off the leaves. Remove the choke and discard; peel the stems. Trim the stems to a length of 1½ to 2 inches. Wipe the cut ends with lemon slices to prevent them from becoming black. Using your fingers, open out the leaves and fill the hollowed center of each with a mixture of chopped mint, garlic, bread crumbs, salt and pepper, moistened with the oil. Push the leaves back into place tightly so that the stuffing remains intact. Arrange the artichokes with the stems facing upward in neat rows in an earthenware dish. Pour the water into the dish, cover it with a sheet of greased waxed paper, then cover the dish tightly. Cook the artichokes in a preheated 400° F. oven for approximately 1 hour. Serve the tender artichokes hot, or cold as an antipasto.

RICE-FILLED PEPPERS

SUMMER STEW OF PEPPERS

(Peperoni al Riso)   Serves 6 to 8

    6 to 8 yellow peppers   2 cups clear stock, heated
    1 onion, sliced   salt and pepper
    ½ cup olive oil   1 mozzarella cheese, diced
    1¼ cups rice   2 tablespoons chopped parsley
    ¼ pound Italian sausage, chopped 1 clove garlic, chopped
    ¼ pound ham, chopped

(Peperonata Estiva)   Serves 6

    2 pounds red and yellow peppers   1 pound tomatoes, peeled, seeded
    ½ cup olive oil   and quartered
    1 pound small white onions   salt

Scorch the peppers over a gas flame, then peel and wash
them. Cut off the tops and set aside. Using a teaspoon, carefully remove the seeds and white bits from inside the peppers.
Cook the onion gently in a skillet with 2 tablespoons of the oil.
Add the rice with ¼ cup more of the oil. Cook the rice lightly,
then add the Italian sausage and the ham. Cover with hot stock
and season with salt and pepper. Cook over high heat, without stirring, until the rice is tender but still firm and the stock
has been absorbed. Remove from the heat, add the mozzarella cheese, parsley and garlic. Stir together gently and stuff
the peppers with this mixture. Replace the top on each pepper
and arrange the peppers in a baking pan with the remainder
of the oil spread on the bottom. Bake in a preheated 350° F.
oven for 20 to 30 minutes. When the peppers are soft and
toasted brown all over, arrange them on a serving dish and
garnish with sprigs of parsley.

Scorch the peppers over a gas flame, peel and remove the
seeds and white bits from the inside. Cut into strips. Heat the
oil in a large skillet, add the strips of pepper and cook them
gently. Peel the onions, blanch them in boiling water for 5
minutes, then drain. Add the onions to the skillet with the
tomatoes. Season with salt and cook the mixture until the
flavors have blended and the sauce thickened. Serve the
pepper stew hot with boiled meats.

STUFFED TOMATOES

STEWED SAVOY CABBAGE, BACON RIND

(Pomodori Farciti)   **Serves 6**

12 plum tomatoes
    salt
½ onion, chopped
¼ cup olive oil
 2 tablespoons dry bread crumbs
 3 anchovies in salt

    lemon slices
 3 hard cooked eggs, finely chopped
 2 ounces ham, diced

(Verze Stufate con Cotenne)   **Serves 6**

2 Savoy cabbages
1 onion, chopped
6 tablespoons olive oil
    salt and pepper

½ cup hot stock
 1 cup dry white wine
¾ to 1 pound bacon rind

Wash and dry the tomatoes, then cut a slice off lengthwise from each tomato. Using a teaspoon, remove the seeds, sprinkle lightly with salt and put the tomatoes upside down in a colander to let the excess liquid drain out. Cook the onion lightly in the oil in a small saucepan. Add the bread crumbs and let them absorb all the onion flavor. Remove the salt from the anchovies with slices of lemon, bone them and finely chop. Put the eggs through a sieve. Add the bread crumbs and anchovies to the eggs, then add the ham. Stir the mixture and stuff the tomatoes with it. Serve the tomatoes cold on a dish lined with lettuce leaves. These tomatoes are excellent served as a summer antipasto, or as a vegetable to accompany a cold supper dish.

Clean the cabbages and cut them into thin strips; wash in plenty of water and drain. Cook the onion lightly in a large skillet with the oil. When it is golden brown, add the cabbage. Season with salt and pepper. Add the hot stock and wine and stew the cabbage, uncovered, for about 30 minutes. Boil the bacon rind briskly in water. Drain when half cooked; cut the rind into julienne and put it in a pot of cold salted water. Bring the water to a boil, and cook until tender. Drain the rind; mix it with the cabbage and cook them together to blend the flavors. For an interesting serving dish, scoop out half of a large squash. Serve the cabbage in this rustic serving dish.

SAUERKRAUT IN WHITE WINE

EGGPLANT PIE

(Crauti al Vino Bianco)　　　　　　　　**Serves 6 to 8**

2¼　pounds sauerkraut
¼　cup olive oil
1　green apple, peeled, cored
　　　and finely sliced
1　onion, chopped
　　salt
2　cups dry white wine
5　juniper berries

(Pasticcio di Melanzane)　　　　　　　　**Serves 6**

2¾　pounds eggplant
　　salt
　　flour
　　cooking oil
1　clove garlic, finely chopped
¼　onion, finely chopped
½　cup olive oil
5　tomatoes, peeled, seeded and
　　chopped
　　pepper
　　chopped basil
　　chopped parsley
2　mozzarella cheeses
　　oregano
5　tablespoons grated Parmesan
　　cheese

Wash the sauerkraut thoroughly in cold water, then drain and squeeze out the excess water. Heat the oil in a large skillet and sauté the apple and onion. Add the sauerkraut, season with salt if necessary and pour in the wine. As soon as the liquid comes to a boil, reduce the heat, cover the saucepan and cook for 1 hour. Just before the end of the cooking time, mix the juniper berries into the sauerkraut. Serve in an oven-proof dish as a vegetable to accompany stuffed pigs' feet or roast pork.

Peel the eggplant and cut them lengthwise into ¼-inch-thick slices. Put them in a colander and sprinkle with salt. Drain for 30 minutes to remove any bitterness. Dry them with a clean cloth, flour each slice and fry in oil heated to 375° F. Remove them from the oil when they are crisp and golden, drain them on absorbent paper and sprinkle with salt. Prepare a marinara sauce by cooking the garlic and onion in the olive oil over low heat. Add the tomatoes and let them simmer gently with the onion and garlic. Season the sauce with salt, pepper, basil and parsley. Grease an oval earthenware dish. Place alternate layers of fried eggplant, spoonfuls of sauce and mozzarella cheese cubes in the dish. Sprinkle every layer with finely chopped basil mixed with parsley and oregano. Finish with a layer of sauce, thin slices of mozzarella and grated Parmesan cheese. Put the dish into a preheated 350° F. oven and when the cheese has melted, sprinkle it with a little olive oil. Bake for about 45 minutes. Serve the eggplant pie from the dish in which it was cooked.

(Fiori di Zucchine Fritti)   **Serves 6**

20 zucchini blossoms	4 eggs, beaten
2 cups flour	cooking oil
1 cup milk	salt

(Cavolfiori e Finocchi alla Panna)   **Serves 6 to 8**

1 cauliflower (about 2¼ pounds)	7 tablespoons butter
salt	1 cup heavy cream
4 heads fennel	1 scant cup grated Parmesan
1 tablespoon flour	cheese
1 onion, chopped	

Remove the blossoms from the squash as soon as they are brought in from the vegetable garden. Open the blossoms and remove the pistils. Wash the blossoms gently to avoid damaging them and lay them on a linen cloth to dry. Prepare the batter by mixing the flour to a smooth paste with the milk. Add the paste to the eggs and mix. For a crisp frying batter, do not add salt at this point. Gently take one blossom at a time and dip it in the batter. Let any excess batter drip off and put the blossom into a pot of oil heated to 375° F., frying only a few at a time. Turn the fritters until they are golden brown and crisp on all sides. Remove with a slotted spoon and drain on absorbent paper. Sprinkle with salt while they are still hot. Arrange the crisp fritters on a serving dish covered with an elegant table napkin and serve immediately.

Remove the leaves and stalk from a very fresh, white cauliflower, separate into flowerets and wash well. Boil the flowerets briskly in a pot of salted water. Drain as soon as the flowerets are cooked but still firm. Remove the outer leaves of the fennel, cut into wedges and boil in salted water with the flour. Drain the fennel as soon as it is tender. Cook the chopped onion in the butter over low heat. When the onion is golden brown, add the cauliflower and fennel and brown them gently. Arrange the browned vegetables in an oven-proof dish, cover with the cream and add salt to taste. Put the dish into a preheated 350° F. oven and cook for about 20 minutes or until the cream has thickened. Sprinkle with grated Parmesan cheese and dot the surface with butter. Brown under the broiler for a few more minutes. Serve piping hot.

SWEET POTATOES IN FOIL

BAKED ONIONS

(Patate Dolci al Cartoccio)   Serves 6

6 sweet potatoes   6 squares aluminum foil

(Cipolle al Forno)   Serves 6

6 medium Bermuda onions   salt and pepper
¼ cup olive oil   2 tablespoons vinegar

Choose sweet potatoes of equal size. Brush them well to remove any dirt, wash and dry them. Roll each potato individually in aluminum foil, twisting both ends to seal them tightly. Arrange them on a baking pan and cook for 1 hour in a preheated 450° F. oven. When the potatoes are soft inside, place them on a dish and serve.

Cut off the roots, peel and boil the onions for a few minutes to keep them white. Plunge them into cold water, drain and put them into a preheated 375° F. oven for about 1 hour. Remove from the oven and cool. Take off the outer layer of the onions and discard. Cut the insides into slices. Arrange the slices in a deep majolica serving dish and season with oil, salt, pepper and vinegar. Serve as an antipasto, as an onion salad or as a vegetable to accompany boiled meats.

STUFFED POTATOES

POTATOES IN HERB-FLAVORED SALT

(Patate Farcite)   Serves 6

  6 *large Idaho potatoes*
     salt
  7 *tablespoons butter*
  ½ *cup heavy cream*

     pepper
     pinch nutmeg
  2 *egg yolks, beaten*

(Patate al Sale Profumato)   Serves 6

2¼ *pounds potatoes*
  5 *tablespoons olive oil*
  7 *tablespoons butter*
     salt
10 *sage leaves, chopped*

     few rosemary sprigs, chopped
  1 *parsley sprig, chopped*
  1 *clove garlic*
     pepper

Choose potatoes uniform in size and shape, wash and boil them in their skins in a small amount of salted water. Cover the pot tightly so that the potatoes cook in their own steam. Proceed with the next step immediately. Using a small knife, cut a thin lengthwise slice from the side of each potato. Gently scoop out the pulp, taking care not to break the skins, and put the shells in a greased oven-proof dish. Put the potato pulp through a food mill and beat in the butter. Add the cream, salt, pepper and a pinch nutmeg. Mix the puréed potato until it is soft and smooth, then put it into a decorator's bag fitted with a wide notched tip. Fill the potato shells with thick swirls of this mixture. Brush the top of the potato mixture with beaten egg yolk and put the potatoes into a preheated 425° F. oven. When the outsides of the potatoes are crisp and golden, remove them from the oven. Serve hot as a first course or as an accompaniment to a roast.

Peel and cube the potatoes. Dry them well in a linen cloth and brown them in a large skillet with the oil and butter. When they are golden brown, put the pan in a preheated 450° F. oven for about 20 minutes to let the potatoes finish cooking. Take enough salt to season the potatoes and flavor it with the chopped sage, rosemary, parsley, a few drops of garlic pressed from a garlic press and pepper. Season the potatoes with this flavored salt as soon as they are taken from the oven; serve immediately.

POTATOES IN MILK

FRIED POTATO CAKE

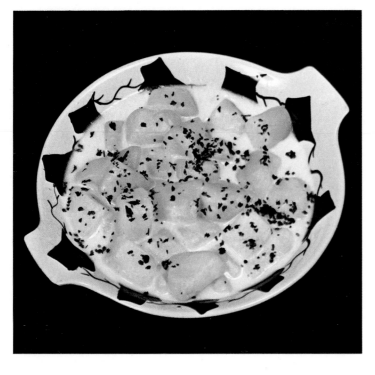

(Patate al Latte)   **Serves 6**

2¼ pounds potatoes	½ cup light cream
salt	1 teaspoon potato flour
4 tablespoons butter	pepper
2 cups milk	2 tablespoons chopped parsley

(Tortino di Patate)   **Serves 6**

2¼ pounds potatoes	3 egg yolks
salt	pinch nutmeg
10 tablespoons butter	5 sage leaves

Wash the potatoes but do not peel them. Boil them in a small amount of salted water. Cover the pot tightly by putting a piece of aluminum foil under the lid. The potatoes will cook in their own steam which prevents loss of flavor and wateriness. Remove from the heat while still firm, peel and cool them. Cut the potatoes into large cubes. Brown the butter in a large saucepan over medium heat. Add the cubed potatoes and brown them. Pour in the milk and cream. Bring to a boil for a few minutes, then thicken the milk sauce with the potato flour dissolved in a little water. When the potatoes are tender, season to taste with salt and pepper. Remove the potatoes from the stove and serve. Sprinkle with chopped parsley.

Peel the potatoes, wash them well and put them in a saucepan with enough water to cook in their own steam. Add a little salt and cover the pan tightly. When they are cooked, put them through a food mill into a bowl containing 6 tablespoons of the butter. Beat the potatoes and butter with a wooden spoon and mix in the egg yolks, one at a time. Add salt if necessary and a pinch nutmeg. Heat the remaining butter in a skillet and sauté the sage leaves. Remove them from the pan and discard. Spread the puréed potatoes over the sizzling butter and shape into a flat round cake. Cook over medium heat, turning the potato cake to brown on both sides. As soon as it is ready, slip onto a round warm serving dish. Serve as an antipasto.

| FRIED POTATOES | POTATO CAKE |

(Patate Fritte)   Serves 6

| 2¼ | pounds potatoes | salt |
| | cooking oil | |

(Patate in Tortiera)   Serves 6

1	pound potatoes	2	onions, finely chopped
¼	pound bacon	5	tablespoons butter
1	cup brown gravy	¾	cup clear stock
	salt and pepper		
2	cloves garlic (inner buds removed), finely chopped		

Peel and wash the potatoes. Cut some of the potatoes into a variety of sizes and shapes—julienne, fluted wafers, small cubes or what you will. Put the potatoes into cold water, then drain them and dry with a cloth. According to size, put them in a wire mesh basket and deep-fry them in oil heated to 375° F. Take them out after a few minutes, when lightly browned; drain. Increase the heat slightly and put them back into the oil for a few minutes. When they are crisp and golden brown, drain them on absorbent paper and sprinkle with salt. Serve on an attractive dish covered with a doily as an accompaniment to roasts or fried dishes.

Peel and wash the potatoes, then cut them into ¼-inch-thick slices. Line a springform cake pan with the bacon. Arrange a layer of potato slices, season with some of the gravy, salt and pepper, then sprinkle with some garlic and onion and dot with butter. Continue making seasoned layers, ending with a layer of potatoes dotted with butter. Put the cake pan into a preheated 375° F. oven for 45 minutes to 1 hour, basting occasionally with spoonfuls of clear stock. When the top is golden brown, remove the potatoes from the oven. Open the pan and slip the cake onto a round serving dish. Serve hot as a simple and economical supper dish.

POTATOES WITH TOMATOES

MUSHROOMS WITH PARSLEY

(Patate al Pomodoro)   Serves 6

2 pounds potatoes
4 tablespoons butter
½ cup olive oil
2 medium onions, chopped

1 pound tomatoes, peeled and
    sliced
salt and pepper
pinch saffron

(Funghi Chiodini al Prezzemolo)   Serves 6

1 pound mushrooms
   lemon slices
¼ onion, chopped
1 clove garlic, chopped
½ cup olive oil

pepper
½ cup dry white wine
salt
2 tablespoons chopped parsley
2 to 3 tablespoons grated Par-
    mesan cheese

Peel and wash the potatoes, then cut them into wedges. Put the wedges into a cloth to dry thoroughly. Heat the butter and oil in a large saucepan and cook the chopped onion lightly until it is golden brown. Add the potatoes and brown. Add the sliced tomatoes, salt, pepper and the saffron dissolved in a small amount of water. Cover the saucepan and cook slowly, adding hot water if the sauce becomes too thick. Taste for seasoning. When the potatoes are cooked, arrange them on a warm dish. Serve as a vegetable.

(Funghi Chiodini are nail-shaped mushrooms unavailable in this country except in cans. Use ordinary fresh mushrooms in this recipe.)

Wipe the mushrooms gently with a damp cloth and rub them with slices of lemon to prevent them from turning black during cooking. Cut into thin slices. Cook the onion and garlic lightly in the olive oil, then increase the heat and add the mushrooms, browning them quickly to dry out all their moisture. Season with pepper. When all the moisture in the mushroom slices is absorbed, pour in the white wine. When the wine evaporates, reduce the heat, cover the saucepan and cook slowly for a very short time. Season the mushrooms with salt and arrange them on a serving dish. Sprinkle them with chopped parsley and grated Parmesan cheese.

BROILED MUSHROOMS

MARINATED MUSHROOMS

(Funghi Porcini alla Griglia)   **Serves 6**

    1 pound mushrooms
      lemon slices
    ½ cup olive oil
    ¼ cup lemon juice
      salt and pepper

    1 clove garlic (inner bud re-
      moved), chopped
    8 tablespoons butter
    2 to 3 tablespoons minced parsley

(Funghi Barboni all'Olio e Limone)   **Serves 6**

    1 pound large mushrooms
      lemon slices
    ½ cup olive oil
      salt and pepper

    1 clove garlic
    ½ cup coarsely grated Parmesan
      cheese

Remove the mushroom stems and use for another dish. Wipe the mushroom caps gently with a damp cloth and rub them with lemon slices. Marinate the mushrooms in the oil, lemon juice, salt, pepper and garlic. Drain the mushrooms after 15 minutes; put them on a very hot broiling rack. Lower the heat after the initial browning and cook them slowly for 5 minutes on each side. As soon as the mushrooms are cooked, baste them with the liquid in which they were marinated. Serve them with the butter, which has been creamed and mixed with the minced parsley and a little salt.

Choose fresh, firm mushrooms. Scrape any traces of earth from the mushrooms, clean and wipe them with a damp cloth, then rub them with slices of lemon. Do not cut off the stems. Cut the mushrooms into very fine "T" slices. Season them in a serving dish with a mixture of oil, salt, pepper and a drop of garlic pressed from a garlic press. Sprinkle with grated Parmesan cheese. Serve this raw mushroom salad as a vegetable, to accompany cold dishes.

MUSHROOMS WITH VEAL KIDNEY

ASPARAGUS WITH WHITE WINE SAUCE

(Champignons con Rognone)   **Serves 6**

1 pound large mushrooms	1 basil sprig, chopped
1 veal kidney	1 parsley sprig, chopped
vinegar	salt and pepper
5 tablespoons olive oil	4 tablespoons butter
2 cloves garlic, chopped	½ cup dry white wine

(Asparagi con Salsa al Vino Bianco)   **Serves 6**

3 pounds asparagus	1½ cups dry white wine
salt	2 tablespoons butter
6 egg yolks	

Choose mushrooms uniform in size and shape and remove the caps. Clean and peel. Clean the stems, chop and reserve for the stuffing. Clean the kidney and remove the external membrane and any traces of fat from the outside and inside. Slice the kidney into a mixture of water and vinegar; drain and dry. Heat the oil and garlic over high heat in a small saucepan and brown the kidney. Arrange the slices of kidney inside the mushroom caps. Cover the kidney with a stuffing made from the chopped mushroom stems mixed with the basil and parsley and seasoned with salt and pepper. Put the stuffed mushrooms in an oven-proof dish and dot each with a little piece of butter. Cook them in a preheated 400° F. oven for 15 to 20 minutes. While the mushrooms are cooking, baste them with white wine and dot with butter. As soon as they are cooked, sprinkle with additional chopped parsley.

Remove the tough ends of the asparagus stalks and discard. Wash and scrape the stalks and trim to the same length. Tie in a bundle and stand the stalks in a tall, narrow pot in salted, cold water which covers about two-thirds the height of the stalks. Cover the pot tightly and boil briskly until the tips begin to bend. Drain them and keep them hot. Put the egg yolks into the top of a double boiler and beat them with the white wine and some salt. Set over warm, but not boiling, water to cook, beating the mixture continually until it is creamy. Before removing it from the heat, add the butter. Arrange the hot asparagus on an oven-proof dish with the tips towards the center. Serve the hot white wine sauce separately. This dish can be used as a main course for lunch.

MUSHROOM PIE

PICKLED MUSHROOMS

(Pasticcio di Funghi Ovoli)   **Serves 6**

2¼ pounds mushrooms
¼ cup olive oil
7 tablespoons butter
2 cloves garlic (inner buds removed),
   chopped
   pepper and salt

4 eggs
1¼ cups grated Parmesan cheese
¼ cup chopped parsley
   slices of buttered bread
2 cups clear stock

(Funghi Porcini sott'Olio)   **Serves 6**

1 pound mushrooms
  water
  vinegar
  salt and pepper

3 or 4 bay leaves
6 peppercorns
  olive oil

Clean the mushrooms carefully. Do not wash them, but scrape the earth from them, peel off any bruised parts and wipe them with a damp cloth. Slice the mushrooms and brown them gently in a large saucepan with 4 tablespoons of the butter and the garlic. Sprinkle with pepper and cook over high heat, shaking the pan, for 10 minutes. Add salt at the end of the cooking time. Beat the eggs, cheese and parsley together; add the mushrooms as soon as they are cooked. Line a deep, round baking dish with some slices of buttered bread, buttered side out. Put half of the mushroom and egg mixture into the bowl, place a layer of bread on top and pour on the remainder of the mushroom mixture. Pour the clear stock slowly over the pie. Let the dish stand for 30 minutes before putting it into a preheated 450° F. oven. Cook for 15 minutes, then turn the pie out on a round serving dish. Sprinkle the top of the mushroom pie with additional grated Parmesan cheese.

Choose small, fresh, firm mushrooms. Remove the earth but do not wash the mushrooms. Scrape the caps and stems and leave them whole. Put them in an earthenware dish with a very little water, vinegar to cover, salt, pepper and a bay leaf. Boil the mushrooms in this liquid for 5 minutes, drain and spread them out on a linen cloth to dry. After a few hours put them into glass jars with 6 peppercorns, 2 or 3 bay leaves and a little salt and cover them with good quality olive oil. Close the jars tightly. Keep in a cool place and wait 3 or 4 days before eating the mushrooms.

ASPARAGUS WITH ROMAINE

ASPARAGUS PIE

(Asparagi alla Lattuga)　　　　　　　　　　**Serves 6**

3 pounds asparagus	⅔ cup lean diced ham
salt	¼ cup clear stock
1 head romaine	pepper
½ onion, sliced	pinch nutmeg
4 tablespoons butter	1 cup heavy cream, warmed

(Asparagi in Tortiera)　　　　　　　　　　**Serves 6**

3 pounds asparagus	pepper
salt	pinch nutmeg
bread, thin slices	3 egg yolks
5 ounces fontina cheese	⅔ cup heavy cream
¼ pound lean bacon (in 1 piece), cubed	

Remove the tough ends of the asparagus stalks and discard. Wash and scrape the stalks and trim to the same length. Tie in a bundle and stand the stalks in a tall, narrow pot in salted cold water which covers about two-thirds the height of the stalks. Cover the pot tightly and boil briskly until the tips begin to bend. Drain and keep hot. Wash the romaine leaves carefully and cut them in half lengthwise. Fold leaves in. Brown the onion in butter and add the ham and romaine. Add the stock and cook for a few minutes. Season with salt, pepper and the nutmeg, then remove from the heat and stir in the warm cream. Arrange the asparagus in an oval oven-proof dish with the tips pointing towards the center of the dish. Pour the romaine sauce over the asparagus and serve immediately.

Remove the tough ends of the asparagus stalks and discard. Wash and scrape the stalks and trim to the same length. Tie in a bundle and stand the stalks in a tall, narrow pot in salted cold water which covers about two-thirds the height of the stalks. Cover the pot tightly and boil briskly until the tips begin to bend. Grease a round layer pan and cover the bottom with bread. Put a layer of sliced fontina cheese on the bread. Arrange the cooked asparagus on this base radially, with the tips pointing towards the center of the pan. Cube the remaining fontina cheese and sprinkle on top with the bacon. Season with salt, pepper and the nutmeg. Mix the egg yolks and cream together in a bowl, then pour the mixture over the asparagus. Put the pan into a preheated 375° F. oven and bake for 25 to 30 minutes or until the surface of the dish is well set and golden brown. Serve hot.

ASPARAGUS WITH CHEESE SAUCE | ASPARAGUS WITH MIMOSA SAUCE

(Asparagi alla Crema)   Serves 6

3 pounds asparagus
    salt
2 cups heavy cream
    pepper

1 cup grated Parmesan cheese
4 egg yolks

(Asparagi alla Salsa Mimosa)   Serves 6

3 pounds asparagus
    salt
4 eggs, hard cooked

8 tablespoons melted butter
5 tablespoons dry bread crumbs
1 tablespoon chopped parsley

Remove the tough ends of the asparagus stalks and discard. Wash and scrape the stalks and trim to the same length. Tie in a bundle and stand the stalks in a tall, narrow pot in salted cold water which covers about two-thirds the height of the stalks. Cover the pot tightly and boil briskly until the tips begin to bend. Drain and keep hot. Boil the cream 1 minute in a large enamel-coated pan, making sure it does not boil over. Remove from the heat and add salt, pepper, grated Parmesan cheese and the egg yolks, mixing in each yolk thoroughly before adding the next. Arrange the asparagus in an earthenware dish with the tips pointing towards the center and season with this creamy sauce.

Remove the tough ends of the asparagus stalks and discard. Wash and scrape the stalks and trim to the same length. Tie in a bundle and stand the stalks in a tall, narrow pot in salted cold water which covers about two-thirds the height of the stalks. Cover the pot tightly and boil briskly until the tips begin to bend. Drain and arrange on a serving dish with the tips pointing towards the center. Cover with a napkin. Shell the hard cooked eggs and put them through a sieve, scattering the yolk and white over the asparagus. Sprinkle the asparagus with a sauce made from the hot melted butter mixed with the bread crumbs, a pinch salt and the chopped parsley.

ASPARAGUS WITH PARMESAN CHEESE | ASPARAGUS WITH OIL AND VINEGAR

(Asparagi alla Parmigiana)   Serves 6

3 pounds asparagus   1¼ cups grated Parmesan cheese
salt   pepper
8 tablespoons butter

(Asparagi all'Olio e Aceto)   Serves 6

3 pounds asparagus   3 tablespoons wine vinegar
salt   pepper
¼ cup olive oil

Remove the tough ends of the asparagus stalks and discard. Wash and scrape the stalks and trim to the same length. Tie in a bundle and stand the stalks in a tall, narrow pot in salted cold water which covers about two-thirds the height of the stalks. Cover the pot tightly and boil briskly until the tips begin to bend; drain. Heat the butter until it melts and turns brown. Arrange the asparagus on a serving dish with the tips pointing towards the center. Sprinkle with the grated Parmesan cheese and then pour the browned butter over. Season the asparagus with salt and pepper to taste. Serve this dish very hot.

Remove the tough ends of the asparagus stalks and discard. Wash and scrape the stalks and trim to the same length. Tie in a bundle and stand the stalks in a tall, narrow pot in salted cold water which covers about two-thirds the height of the stalks. Cover the pot tightly and boil briskly until the tips begin to bend. Drain and arrange on a serving dish, with the tips pointing towards the center. Serve the asparagus salad with a dressing made by mixing together the oil, wine vinegar, salt and pepper.

Sweets and Desserts

The recipes that appear here are those most easily made at home. Yet they reiterate the classical themes of Italian sweets, from pastry cookies to zabaglione. When a mother initiates her daughter into the art of cooking, she often begins with the preparation of a cake. The choice of recipes has been made with this in mind and should appeal especially to young people. Italian-American cooks have adapted many traditional Italian recipes to suit the palates of Americans and they have done so with notable success. The recipes here include both traditional Italian desserts and sweets and cakes adapted by the Italian-American communities.

SOVEREIGN OR SUPREME CAKE   SACHER TORTE

(Torta Sovrana)   Serves 6

    2 cups (7 ounces) shelled almonds   2 egg yolks
    ⅔ cup sugar   ⅛ teaspoon salt
    ¼ ounce package dry yeast   ⅓ cup heavy cream
    1¾ cups all-purpose flour   1 egg, beaten
    ⅔ cup butter, softened

(Torta Sacher)   Serves 6

    6 eggs, separated   ¼ cup apricot preserves, sieved
    ¾ cup sugar   2 tablespoons rum
    2 cups all-purpose flour   11 ounces semisweet chocolate
    1 teaspoon baking powder   milk
    ½ cup powdered cocoa   confectioners' sugar

Blanch the almonds in boiling water and remove their skins. Pound the almonds in a mortar with a pestle or grind them to a fine powder in an electric blender. Place the flour on a pastry board and crumble the yeast in a little lukewarm water to dissolve it. Make a well in the center. Put the butter, egg yolks, salt, cream and yeast into the well. Work the flour into these ingredients with the hands to form a smooth and pliable dough. Add the sugar, form the mixture into a ball and let the dough stand for 1 hour, covered with a floured cloth, until it has risen. Roll out the dough to a thickness of ¼ of an inch. Grease a 9- to 10-inch round layer pan and sprinkle it with sugar. Line the pan with the dough, reserving some for the lattice top. Cover the dough with the crushed almonds. Cut the reserved dough into strips and form a lattice on top of the cake. Brush the surface of the cake with beaten egg and bake it in a preheated 350° F. oven for about 35 minutes or until it is golden brown.

Put the egg yolks and sugar into a bowl and mix with a wooden spoon until the mixture is light and frothy. Beat the egg whites until they are thick and stand in peaks. Mix together the flour, baking powder and cocoa; blend into the egg yolk mixture, stirring constantly. Add the beaten egg whites gradually, a spoonful at a time, folding them in gently. Butter and flour a 9-inch cake pan, 2 inches deep. Pour the mixture into the pan and bake in preheated 350° F. oven for about 30 minutes or until a wooden pick inserted into it comes out dry. Remove it from the oven and cool on a cake rack for 10 minutes. Turn out of the pan and when it is completely cool, cut it into three layers. Spread the first layer with some of the apricot preserves and place the second layer on top. Sprinkle with rum and spread with the remaining preserves. Place the third layer on top and cover it with chocolate icing made by melting the chocolate with a little milk and confectioners' sugar in the top of a double boiler. Spread the icing over the top and sides of the cake. Decorate the surface of the cake with a meshwork of thin lines of icing.

SWEET NOTHINGS

MONT BLANC

(Chiacchiere—Galani o Nastri)   Serves 6

3½ cups all-purpose flour
3 eggs
4 tablespoons butter, softened
½ cup sugar
⅛ teaspoon salt
rind of 2 oranges, grated
rind of 1 lemon, grated
½ cup white wine
cooking oil
vanilla-flavored confectioners' sugar

(Monte Bianco)   Serves 6

2½ pounds chestnuts
2 quarts milk
3½ cups confectioners' sugar
rum
1 quart heavy cream

These "knots" are made in many households at carnival time. Put the flour on a pastry board and make a well in the middle of it. Put the eggs, butter, sugar, salt, orange and lemon rinds and wine into the well. Work all the ingredients together into a ball of dough and let it stand for 1 hour. Roll the pastry out wafer thin. Cut some of the dough into strips with a pastry wheel, knotting the pieces as if they were ribbons. Cut the remaining pastry into squares or rectangles and make a little cut in the center of each. Fry the pastry quickly in hot (370° F.) oil to cover, a few pieces at a time. When they are golden brown, take them out with a slotted spoon. Drain and cool on absorbent paper. Sprinkle the pastry with vanilla-flavored confectioners' sugar. Pile them on a large tray and serve.

Cut a cross on the flat side of each chestnut. Put them in a pan, cover with water and bring to a boil. Remove from the heat and shell and peel the chestnuts while still hot. Put the peeled chestnuts into the milk and cook until tender. When cooked and still hot, drain off milk and discard. Put chestnuts through a food mill into a bowl. Add the confectioners' sugar and rum to taste to the puréed chestnuts. Mix well to blend the flavors. Sieve this mixture, letting the purée fall in the center of a round serving dish, shaping it with hands into a cone shape. Whip the cream until it is thick and sweeten it with additional confectioners' sugar. Cover the chestnut cone with the whipped cream to make it look like fallen snow.

(Torta San Remigio)   **Serves 6**

10 eggs, separated	2 tablespoons dry bread crumbs
1¾ cups sugar	10 ounces mascarpone cheese
½ cup butter	scant cup vanilla-flavored
3½ cups all-purpose flour	confectioners' sugar
1 teaspoon baking powder	

(Dolcetti della Nonna)   **Serves 6**

7 tablespoons egg whites (3 to 4 eggs)	1 cup mascarpone or ricotta cheese
1¾ cups confectioners' sugar	3 tablespoons sugar
¼ cup shelled almonds	¼ cup brandy
10 ounces red chestnuts, chopped	1 sheet prepared sponge layer cake
2 tablespoons butter	10½ ounces semisweet chocolate
¼ cup rum	¼ cup water
1 cup chopped cashew nuts	toasted filberts
grated chocolate	
chopped toasted almonds	

Beat the egg yolks and sugar in a copper bowl until the mixture is soft and frothy. Soften the butter over hot water. Sift the flour with the baking powder into the butter and add the mixture to the egg yolks and sugar, stirring constantly. Beat the egg whites until they stand in peaks. Gradually fold them into the yolk mixture. Butter a round 8-inch pan, and an 8-inch square pan, then coat them with bread crumbs. Divide the mixture between the two pans and bake in a preheated 350° F. oven for 35 to 40 minutes. Turn out onto a cake rack. When the cakes are cool, cut the square one into ½-inch cubes. Divide the other cake into two layers. Prepare a cream filling by beating the mascarpone cheese and the vanilla-flavored sugar with a wooden spoon until creamy. Spread most of this filling on one of the layers and place it on a serving dish. Top with the second layer and spread with the remaining filling. Pyramid the cake cubes on top of the cake and sprinkle with confectioners' sugar.

Beat the egg whites and half of the confectioners' sugar with a whisk in a small copper bowl. Add the remaining confectioners' sugar slowly, beating constantly until stiff. Blanch the ¼ cup of almonds in boiling water and remove the skins. Toast them on a baking sheet in a preheated 325° F. oven for 10 to 15 minutes or until lightly browned. Chop them finely and fold them slowly into the stiff egg whites. Fill paper muffin pan liners with the meringue and bake in a preheated 300° F. oven for about 45 minutes. Purée the red chestnuts and work in the butter, rum and cashew nuts. Shape the mixture into little balls and roll half of them in grated chocolate and half in chopped toasted almonds. Beat the cheese, 3 tablespoons of sugar and the brandy with a wooden spoon. Cut the sponge cake into neat rectangles and spread half of them with the cheese cream. Sandwich with the remaining rectangles. Heat the semisweet chocolate and water in a double boiler. When the chocolate is melted and lukewarm, dip the spongecake sandwiches into it, using a spoon to coat them completely. Decorate the tops of the chocolate-covered cakes with toasted filberts. Arrange the cakes on a three-tiered cake stand.

CAKE WITH FRUIT

CHOCOLATE CUSTARD TART

(Torta di Frutta)   **Serves 6**

For the cake

5 eggs	1¾ cups all-purpose flour
1 cup sugar	¼ cup melted butter
1½ teaspoons baking powder	½ teaspoon vanilla

For the filling

5 egg yolks	⅓ cup flour
⅔ cup sugar	liqueur to taste
2 cups milk	1 cup pitted cherries
grated rind of 1 lemon	

To prepare the cake: Beat the eggs and sugar in a bowl with a whisk until the mixture is light and frothy. Sift the flour and baking powder and stir it into the eggs lightly with the butter and vanilla. Butter a 9-inch cake pan and coat it with sugar. Pour the cake mixture into it and bake in 350° F. oven for 30 minutes. As soon as the cake is done, remove it from the pan and cool on a cake rack. Split the cake into two layers, trimming the edge of one layer to make it smaller than the other.
To prepare the filling: Beat the egg yolks and sugar together in a small copper bowl. Heat the milk and grated lemon rind together. Stir the flour into the egg yolks, then slowly add the milk. Thicken the filling over medium heat, stirring constantly, and simmer for a few minutes. Cool. Put the larger of the two layers on a serving dish and soak it with liqueur. Spread a thick layer of the filling on it and place cherries around the edge. Soak the smaller layer in liqueur. Cover it with the remaining cream and lay it on top of the larger layer. Place a few cherries on top of the cake.

(Doposcuola per Bambini)   **Serves 6**

⅓ recipe short crust pastry cookies (page 275)	2 tablespoons unsweetened powdered cocoa
5 egg yolks	20 ladyfingers
⅔ cup sugar	⅓ cup sweet marsala
2 cups milk	20 Bing cherries, pitted
grated rind of 1 lemon	1 egg yolk, beaten
⅓ cup all-purpose flour	

Prepare the sweet short crust pastry and let it rest. Roll it out to about ¼ inch in thickness. Reserve some of the pastry for the lattice topping on the cake. Butter a 10-inch springform pan and line it with the pastry, making sure that the pastry fits closely to the bottom and sides of the pan. Beat the egg yolks and sugar in a copper pot steadily for about 5 minutes. Heat the milk and grated lemon rind together. Stir the flour into the egg yolks, then very slowly stir in the hot milk. Put the pot over medium heat, stirring constantly, until the mixture thickens. Cool and stir in the cocoa. Pour half of the filling into the pastry-lined pan. Dip the ladyfingers in the marsala, then lay them on the filling; cover with the remaining filling. Cut the reserved pastry into strips and arrange on top of the filling in a lattice pattern. Place a cherry in the center of each "diamond." Put the cake into a preheated 450° F. oven and reduce the heat to 350° F. About 30 minutes through the cooking time remove the cake from the oven and brush it with the egg yolk to glaze it. Return the cake to the oven until it is golden brown (about 10-15 minutes longer). Cool before removing it from the pan.

ARIANNA PUDDING

(Budino Arianna)   Serves 6

3 eggs	½ cup golden seedless raisins
⅓ cup sugar	¼ cup rum
2 cups milk	½ recipe Zabaglione (page 282)
1 vanilla bean	¼ cup heavy cream, whipped
¼ pound prepared sponge cake	1 candied orange
1½ cups (10½ ounces) diced mixed candied fruit	

Beat the eggs and sugar together for about 5 minutes. Scald the milk and vanilla bean together. Remove the bean and pour the hot milk very slowly into the beaten eggs, stirring constantly. Grease a 5- to 6-cup mold and coat it with sugar. Fill it with alternate layers of sponge cake, candied fruit and raisins that have been soaked in rum. When the mold is nearly full, pour the custard mixture in, a little at a time. Put the mold in a pan with 1 inch of hot water and bake in a preheated 350° F. oven for about 1 hour or until the pudding is set; do not let the water boil. Allow the pudding to cool completely before turning it out onto an elegant serving dish. Prepare the zabaglione and when it is cool, gently fold in the whipped cream. Pour the zabaglione over the pudding and decorate with the candied orange.

WHIPPED CREAM CAKE

(Torta alla Panna)   Serves 6

3 eggs	¼ cup melted butter
⅔ cup sugar	dry bread crumbs
1¼ cups all-purpose flour	2 cups heavy cream
⅓ cup arrowroot flour or corn flour	candied fruit
2½ teaspoons baking powder	grated chocolate

Beat the eggs and sugar together for about 5 minutes. Sift the flour in gradually with the arrowroot flour or corn flour and baking powder. Pour in the melted butter. Butter an 8-inch cake pan and coat with dry bread crumbs. Pour the cake mixture into it and bake it in a preheated 350° F. oven for about 30 minutes. Remove the cake from the pan to dry and cool on a cake rack. Split the cake into two layers. Whip the cream until stiff and fill the layers with half of it. Put the remaining whipped cream into a decorator's bag fitted with a fluted tip and decorate the surface of the cake with piped roses and swirls of cream. Decorate the cake with candied fruit and grated chocolate.

PLUM AND APRICOT TART

MIXED FRUIT SALAD CAKE

(Crostata di Prugne e Albicocche)   **Serves 6**

2¼ cups all-purpose flour	⅛ teaspoon salt
¾ cup plus 2 tablespoons butter, softened	ladyfingers
	jam
½ cup sugar	plums, halved and pitted
1 egg	apricots, halved and pitted
grated rind of 1 lemon	

(Torta di Macedonia di Frutta)   **Serves 6**

2¼ cups all-purpose flour	⅛ teaspoon salt
¾ cups butter, softened	prepared sponge cake slices
½ cup sugar	apricot jam
1 egg	fruit in season

Place the flour on a pastry board and make a well in the center. Put the butter, sugar, egg, grated lemon rind and salt into the well, and work in the flour, leaving a little on the board. Form the dough into a ball and let it rest on the board for 1 hour, covered with a cloth. At the end of this time, roll it out to a thickness of slightly less than ¼ inch. Line a 10-inch non-stick springform cake pan with the pastry, pressing it to the sides and bottom to make it fit well. Prick the pastry with a fork to prevent it from puffing. Bake it in a preheated 375° F. oven for 15-20 minutes, or until the pastry is golden brown. Remove the side of the pan and let the shell cool on a cake rack. When it is cold, fill it with alternate layers of lady fingers and raspberry jam. Arrange the plums and apricots on the final layer of ladyfingers, then slip the tart gently onto a serving dish.

Place the flour on a pastry board and make a well in the center. Put the butter, sugar, egg, grated lemon rind and salt into the well. Mix the ingredients together with a fork and work in the flour, leaving a little on the board. Form the pastry into a ball and let rest on the board for 1 hour. Roll the pastry out to a thickness of slightly less than ½ inch. Line a non-stick, springform cake pan with the pastry, pressing it well into the bottom and sides of the pan. Prick the pastry with a fork to prevent it from puffing. Bake it in a preheated 375° F. oven for 15-20 minutes or until golden brown. Remove the pastry shell from the pan and cool on a cake rack. When it is cold, fill it with slices of sponge cake spread with apricot jam. Decorate the surface with fruit. This tart has a slice of pineapple in the middle surrounded by peach slices, cherries and half apricots. Garnish with toasted nuts. Grapes and apple slices can also be used to decorate this cake.

(Pasta Frolla)   Serves 6

6¼ cups all-purpose flour	grated rind of 1 lemon
2⅔ cups butter, softened	½ teaspoon salt
1⅓ cups sugar	confectioners' sugar
3 egg yolks	

(Tortellini di Marmellata)   Serves 6

2 cups all-purpose flour	⅛ teaspoon salt
¾ cup butter, softened	quince preserves
½ cup sugar	1 egg, beaten
2 eggs	confectioners' sugar
grated rind of 1 lemon	

Place the flour on a pastry board and make a well in the center. Put the butter, sugar, egg yolks, grated lemon rind and salt into the well. Work the flour in gently with the hands and form into a large ball. Cover with a towel and put in a cool place to rest for about 1 hour. Roll the dough out to a thickness of ¼ inch and cut into different shapes with cutters. Place the cookies well apart on a baking sheet and bake them in a preheated 375° F. oven for 10 to 15 minutes. As soon as they are golden brown, remove the cookies from the oven and cool on a cake rack before sprinkling with confectioners' sugar.

Place the flour on a pastry board and make a well in the center. Put the butter, sugar, 2 eggs, grated lemon rind and salt into the well. Work the flour in gently with the hands and form into a ball. Cover with a towel and let rest for 1 hour on the pastry board. Roll out the pastry to a thickness of ¼ inch and cut out circles 3 inches in diameter. In the center of each circle put ½ teaspoon quince preserves. Brush the inside edge with remaining beaten egg and fold the pastry circle over to form a half circle. Press with the fingers to seal. Alternatively, increase the amount of preserves, brush the edges of two circles with beaten egg, put one circle on top of another and seal. Place the turnovers on a baking sheet, brush with beaten egg and bake in a preheated 350° F. oven for 10 to 15 minutes. Remove them from the oven and serve. Sprinkle with confectioners' sugar if desired.

FRUIT BREAD

(Pane di Frutta)   Serves 6

⅔ cup butter, softened	1¼ cups arrowroot flour
2 cups confectioners' sugar	2 teaspoons baking powder
2 eggs	1 cup golden seedless raisins
2 egg yolks	⅓ cup diced candied orange
1⅓ cups all-purpose flour	peel

Cream the butter and confectioners' sugar in a bowl with a wooden spoon until soft and fluffy. Beat in eggs and egg yolks one at a time, beating well after each addition. Mix the flour, arrowroot and baking powder together and gradually beat into batter. Fold in golden raisins and candied orange peel. Butter a 9 x 5 x 3-inch loaf pan and coat it with a mixture of 1 tablespoon granulated sugar and dry bread crumbs. Pour the dough into the pan. Bake the cake in a preheated 350° F. oven for about 1 hour or until a wooden pick inserted in the center comes out clean. Remove from the pan and cool on a cake rack. Decorate the top of the cake with a strip of confectioners' sugar along each side. Serve on a rectangular dish and cut into slices.

ALMOND CAKE

(Torta di Mandorle)   Serves 6

1 cup (3.5 ounces) shelled almonds	¾ cup plus 2 tablespoons sugar
¾ cup plus 2 tablespoons all-purpose flour	½ cup melted butter
	20 whole almonds, peeled

Blanch the almonds in boiling water, then remove the skins. Dry them in a preheated 325° F. oven and chop them finely. Mix together the flour and sugar, add the butter and chopped almonds and mix into a dough; do not overhandle. Let stand in a bowl covered with a towel for 1 hour. Butter an 8-inch round layer pan and coat with 1 tablespoon sugar. With your fingertips spread the dough in the pan pressing it up along the side of the pan to form a rim. Decorate the cake with the whole almonds and bake in a 375° F. oven for about 30 minutes.

COUNTRY-STYLE CAKE

APPLE CAKE

(Focaccia Rustica)   Serves 6

1¼ cups butter, softened	½ teaspoon vanilla
1¼ cups sugar	2 packets dried yeast
4 eggs	¾ cup warm milk
1 teaspoon salt	7 cups all-purpose flour
grated rind of 1 lemon	coarse sugar

(Torta di Mele)   Serves 6

1¼ cups plus 1 tablespoon milk, lukewarm	4 eggs
1 packet dried yeast	grated rind of 1 lemon
⅔ cup butter, softened	½ teaspoon vanilla
1⅓ cups sugar	4 cups plus 2 tablespoons all-purpose flour, sifted
1 teaspoon salt	4 apples, peeled and sliced

Cream the butter and sugar together with a wooden spoon. Beat in the eggs, one at a itme. Then stir in the salt, grated lemon rind, vanilla and the yeast dissolved in the warm milk until blended. Work in the flour. Form the dough into a ball and let it stand, covered with a towel, in a warm place for 1 hour. At the end of this time, knead the dough until it is smooth and elastic. Shape it into a long thick roll and join the ends to form a doughnut shape. Put the dough on a floured baking sheet. Firmly seal the joint of the circle by moistening and pressing it with the fingers. Sprinkle with coarse sugar and bake in a preheated 350° F. oven for about 40 minutes. Let the cake cool before cutting it.

Dissolve yeast in lukewarm milk. Cream butter with the sugar and salt until fluffy. Beat in the eggs one at a time and then the grated lemon rind and vanilla. Stir in the milk mixture, a spoonful at a time, and finally stir in the sifted flour. Mix all the ingredients together well and let the dough stand in a bowl covered with a cloth for about 45 minutes or until risen. Butter and flour a 10-inch springform cake pan. Spoon half of the dough into the pan and lay half of the apple slices on top. Cover with the remaining dough. Arrange the remaining apple slices on the top. Bake the cake in a preheated 350° F. oven for about 30 to 40 minutes or until it is golden brown. Turn out and cool the cake on a cake rack before serving.

APRICOTS WITH WHIPPED CREAM

COLD ZABAGLIONE

(Albicocche alla Panna)   Serves 6

½ cup water
1 cup sugar
10 large ripe apricots, halved and pitted
2 cups heavy cream
¾ cup confectioners' sugar
¼ cup maraschino liqueur
    small macaroons

(Zabaione Freddo)   Serves 6

6 egg yolks
⅔ cup sugar
¾ cup sweet marsala
    grated rind of ½ lemon
⅛ teaspoon cinnamon
¼ teaspoon vanilla
¾ cup heavy cream, whipped

Boil the water and sugar in a saucepan to form a syrup. Add the apricots and let soak for 5 minutes. Whip the cream, gradually beating in the confectioners' sugar until stiff. Pour the liqueur into a wide plate and soak the macaroons in it. Fill a decorator's bag with some of the whipped cream. Pipe the cream into the hollow center of each apricot in the shape of a rose. Arrange the apricots on a round dish and put the remaining whipped cream in the center of the dish, garnished with a few macaroons. Place a macaroon on top of each cream-covered apricot and serve.

Beat the egg yolks and sugar in a bowl or the top of a double boiler until the yolks are light and frothy. Add the marsala, grated lemon rind, cinnamon and vanilla. Put the bowl or top of a double boiler over hot water, beating the eggs constantly; do not allow the water to boil. As soon as the zabaglione swells up and is light and even in texture, remove it from the heat but continue stirring it until cool. Gently add the whipped cream. Chill. Serve the zabaglione in individual dishes, accompanied by cookies. Garnish each zabaglione with a rose-shaped swirl of whipped cream topped with a glacéed fruit.

BAKED PEACHES

MARRONS COUPÉ

(Pesche al Forno)   Serves 6

6 peaches, semiripe, halved and pitted	1 cup white wine
¼ pound macaroons	½ cup sugar
¼ cup almond liqueur	2 egg yolks
peach leaves	12 blanched almonds

(Coppa di Marrons Glacés)   Serves 6

2 cups heavy cream	2½ ounces chocolate sprinkles
¾ cup confectioners' sugar	¾ cup pistachio nuts, chopped
10 ounces marrons glacés	

Scoop out a little of the center of each peach with a teaspoon, reserve this pulp in a small bowl. Crush the macaroons and soak them in the liqueur. Soak the peach leaves in the white wine. Mix the crushed macaroons with the reserved peach pulp. Add the sugar and egg yolks and mix together. Spoon a tablespoonful of this filling into each peach center and decorate with a blanched almond. Butter a baking pan lightly and lay the peaches on it, keeping them separated from each other. Discard the peach leaves; pour the white wine over the peaches and bake them in a preheated 350° F. oven for about 30 minutes.

Whip the cream, gradually beating in confectioners' sugar until it is stiff. Reserve six of the *marrons glacés* and chop the rest. Put them into individual serving dishes and cover with some of the whipped cream. Decorate each dish with a whole *marron glacé* and garnish with the chocolate sprinkles and pistachio nuts. Serve the remainder of the whipped cream in a separate dish.

PEACH AND RICE PUDDING

RICOTTA CHEESECAKE

(Dolce di Pesche al Forno)   Serves 6

  4 cups milk
  ¼ cup sugar
  ½ teaspoon vanilla
  ⅛ teaspoon salt
  1 tablespoon butter

  1 cup rice
  1 can peach slices, drained
  ¼ cup apricot preserves
    candied cherries
    toasted pistachio nuts

(Torta di Ricotta)   Serves 6

  1 pound ricotta or cottage cheese
  ½ cup sugar
    grated rind of 1 lemon
  4 egg yolks
  ½ cup all-purpose flour

  ⅓ cup golden seedless raisins
  ½ cup candied fruit, finely
    chopped
  2 egg whites

Scald the milk, then add the sugar, vanilla, salt and butter. Stir together, then add the rice and cook for about 20 minutes. When the milk is absorbed, let the rice cool. Spread it out on a round serving dish and decorate the center and edge of the pudding with peach slices. Cover it with a layer of apricot preserves and garnish with candied cherries and toasted pistachio nuts.

Sieve the ricotta or cottage cheese into a bowl. Work in the sugar and grated lemon rind. Add the egg yolks one at a time, then the flour, raisins and candied fruit. Beat the egg whites until stiff; fold them gently into the cheese mixture. Butter a 9-inch round layer pan 2 inches deep and coat it with sugar and bread crumbs. Pour the cake mixture into the pan and bake in a preheated 350° F. oven for about 30 minutes. When ready, remove the cake from the oven. Let it cool, then turn it out onto a silver plate.

Photo Giorgio Lotti

CANDELAUS COOKIES

FILBERT CAKE

(Candelaus)   Serves 6

1¼ pounds shelled almonds	2 cups confectioners' sugar
2 cups granulated sugar	grated rind of 2 lemons
⅔ cup water	¼ cup orange water

(Torta alle Nocciole)   Serves 6

½ pound shelled filbert nuts	½ cup milk
1¾ cups all-purpose flour	2 teaspoons baking powder
½ cup corn flour	⅓ cup golden seedless raisins
1½ cups sugar	grated lemon rind
⅔ cup powdered cocoa	3 tablespoons apricot preserves
⅔ cup melted butter	½ pound almonds, finely chopped
6 eggs	

Blanch the almonds in boiling water, peel them and put them in a warm oven to dry. Chop them very finely or pulverize them in an electric blender. Heat the granulated sugar with the water in a copper pan. When the sugar has dissolved, add the confectioners' sugar and almonds. Add the lemon rind and orange water. Cook for 5 minutes and when the mixture comes away from the bottom of the pan in a compact mass, remove it from the stove and let it cool slightly. With a spoon, press this spun sugar mixture into a variety of cookie cutters, smoothing with wet hands. Put the cookies on a lightly greased baking sheet and cook in a 425° oven for 5 minutes. Dissolve some sugar in a very small quantity of water *to* make a syrup. Paint the candelaus cookies with this syrup to give them a shiny appearance.

Place the filberts in a preheated 350° F. oven for 10 to 15 minutes. Cool slightly and rub off the skins. Chop the nuts finely. Place the flour and corn flour in a bowl. Mix in the sugar, cocoa, chopped nuts and butter. Stir in the eggs one at a time. Add the milk, baking powder, raisins and the lemon rind. Mix all the ingredients together well. Butter a 10-inch pan 2 inches deep and coat with a mixture of 1 tablespoon each of flour and sugar. Pour the cake mixture into the pan and place it in a preheated 350° F. oven for about 30 minutes. The cake is ready when a wooden pick inserted in the center comes out clean. Remove it from the pan and cool completely on a cake rack. Spread the top and sides of the cake with apricot preserves and cover it with a layer of very finely chopped almonds.

NOODLE CAKE

RICE CAKE

(Torta di Tagliatelle)   **Serves 6**

3½ cups all-purpose flour
 5 eggs
 2 tablespoons maraschino liqueur
 1 tablespoon lukewarm water
 ½ pound shelled almonds
 ¼ pound macaroons

1¼ cups sugar
 1 teaspoon vanilla
 ½ cup melted butter
 ⅓ recipe short crust pastry
    cookies (page 275)

(Torta di Riso)   **Serves 6 to 8**

 4 cups milk
 1 teaspoon vanilla
 ½ cup sugar
 ½ teaspoon salt
 1 cup rice
 1 tablespoon butter

 6 egg yolks
 ¼ pound candied orange peel,
    finely chopped
 ⅓ recipe short crust pastry
    cookies (page 275)

Place the flour on a pastry board and make a well in the center. Put the eggs, maraschino and lukewarm water into the well. Mix the ingredients together to form a stiff dough. Knead it well until it is smooth and elastic. Cover and let stand 30 minutes. Roll it out until it is wafer thin. Let it dry. Roll the dough up into a cylinder and cut it into fine strips which can be opened out gently. Blanch the almonds in boiling water, peel, toast in the oven and chop them very finely. Crush the macaroons and add them to the chopped almonds, together with the sugar and vanilla. Line an 8-inch buttered springform cake pan with short crust pastry and sprinkle it with a mixture of flour and sugar. Put a layer of the noodles on the bottom of the pastry lined pan. Sprinkle a tablespoonful of the almond mixture over it. Continue alternating layers of noodles and almond mixture, finishing with a layer of noodles. Pour the melted butter over the top and bake the cake in a preheated 350° F. oven for about 30 minutes. Remove the cake from the oven and serve it while still warm.

Scald the milk, then add the vanilla, sugar and salt. Stir in the rice and cook for about 20 minutes or until the milk is absorbed. Add the butter to the rice to give it a shiny texture. Cool and then stir in egg yolks one at a time. Add the candied orange peel. Mix well and pour the rice mixture into a 10-inch springform cake pan lined with short crust pastry. Bake in a preheated 375° F. oven for about 25 minutes or until knife inserted in center of custard comes out clean. Serve hot.

Index

Photo Giorgio Lotti